Trusting the Universe

Life Lessons

Larry Walsh, Sr.

Trusting the Universe: Life Lessons

By Larry Walsh, Sr.

© Copyright Larry Walsh, Sr., 2020

Mission Point Press
2554 Chandler Road
Traverse City, Michigan 49696
www.MissionPointPress.com
231-421-9513

Cover photo courtesy of Larry Walsh, Sr.
Cover design by Heather Shaw

Printed in the United States of America

ISBN: 978-1-950659-90-6
Library of Congress Control Number: 2020923592

Table of Contents

Welcome

They didn't seem like blessings at the time, but I have had many blessings sent my way. The first time I was blessed was when I was born into a large Irish family on Chicago's South Side, with seven brothers and two sisters. Having that many people in one house was, to say the least, busy. One of the fondest memories I have of my early childhood was at night when my brothers and I went to bed. At the time, there were six of us boys. Our bedroom was an unfinished attic with our beds lined up next to each other barracks-style. No walls between us. No air conditioning and no heat. It was very hot in the summer and very cold in the winter.

For as hot or cold it was in our attic bedroom, this time together with my brothers was special. Lying side-by-side in our beds, we would talk about what had happened for each of us that day, and about all our future dreams.

My next blessing came when "I" became "we"– when I met Debbie and she became my life-long partner and my wife. As a bubbly young blonde, Debbie took my breath away. It didn't take long for me to find out that her beauty was not only external, but internal as well. Our partnership eventually brought us four children of our own. Debbie and I were blessed a third time as our children have grown into fine adults and have given us 14 grandchildren.

Our life experiences shape who we are, and my experiences have given me the stories that have formed the person I am today. As I grew, and as my children and then grandchildren got older, I began to share some of those life stories with them. I'd tell them about the time I met their mother or grandmother, or share stories about my early childhood and what it was like growing up in a family of twelve people. I'd tell them what it felt like to get my first bike, or witnessing my mother and father struggle, without weakening, to keep our big family in food and clothes. I'd tell them about how I ended up in information technology, or how devastating it was to lose a business. I'd tell about raising four children and the lessons our kids taught me. I'd share even the hard stories about losing loved ones and how I dealt with those feelings of loss.

I often found myself ending these tales by telling the kids or grandkids about what lessons I'd learned. More than once during story time, one of them would say, "Dad, you should write down these stories. Maybe as a book." It was that encouragement that led me here.

Writing requires solitude, I've found. But with a 50-year career of 50-hour workweeks, along with the hours devoted to an active family, I never really had much "alone time" that I could put toward writing, which was fine – Debbie would often tell me that I "don't do 'alone' very well." Now that I'm retired, I've had the time to reflect on this lifetime of rich experiences, and time to write them down.

My purpose with this book is to share some of these stories and insights with family, friends, and those readers I may not have met yet. In reflecting on what I've learned along the way, I wish I could say I learned my lessons in real time, while the events were happening. But I can't say that. I found that my lessons were often lost in the moment, and I didn't appreciate the wisdom being revealed until later when I had time to reflect. By taking time to reflect on those lessons, I learned things that helped form me and helped guide me in relating to people, with colleagues on the job, or with the members of my family.

These stories are all true to the best of my recollection. I have changed names only to respect the anonymity of friends who may have viewed these "learning experiences" differently than I did.

As I brought these stories together over many months, I was able to reflect on the nature of memory. As I reached into the past for well-told stories, I found that more stories kept popping up – each standing in line and clamoring to be told. Even now as I write, other stories of life events keep rising into memory, wanting to also be put on stage. I added to the list as long as I could, but this book can only be so long. Some stories will have to wait for the next book.

I hope you enjoy reading these tales as much as I have enjoyed living them and now telling them. I've always felt fulfillment in helping others. If sharing these stories of learning, of mistakes made or successes enjoyed, if any one of these stories can help someone find their way through a tough situation, I'll say it's been a worthwhile effort for me.

Sending love to all those who have arrived here.

Bonding with a brother

"Do you want to help me with my paper route?"
When I was five years old, my oldest brother Jim, who was exactly 5½ years older than me, had a morning paper route. The job meant getting up at 5:00 a.m. when the papers got delivered to the house, rolling the papers, and then heading out to deliver them to houses in the neighborhood.

Jim asked me if I would like to help him on his paper route. It was a lot of responsibility for a five-year-old, but I said sure. *Any chance to spend time with an older brother is a great opportunity.* I can still feel the sleep leaving my eyes when he would shake me awake. The fresh smell of morning air is engraved in my memory—it's probably why I am still a "morning person" today.

Every morning my brother and I would be out the door shortly after 5:00, deliver the papers, and be back home in time to get ready for school. While it seemed like a reasonable job for two kids back then, I can't see my grandsons, age 10 and five, going out on their own at 5:00 a.m. every day. But that's what we did.

It might sound strange, but one of my fondest memories about delivering papers was the biting-cold air of dark winter mornings. Sometimes the bitter cold made my face feel like it would crack, and the snow was often too high to ride our bikes to make our deliveries. I guess the cold made me feel alive? I know it would wake me up quickly. Sometimes it would get so cold that my brother would bring out some matches to light the contents of a garbage can on fire to help us warm up. My brother was always watching out for me. If the snow was deep or I started to get tired, he would load me and the newspapers onto a sled – and drag us across the snow from house to house.

Working that early morning paper route with my brother taught me a few things, even as a five-year-old. I learned that self-responsibility and meeting that delivery commitment each day was important. I learned about the value of companionship. Working this pre-dawn paper route together let my brother and me get to know each other really well, and we remained close until he was called to his rest many decades later.

I'm not sure how much help a five-year-old can be on a paper route, but I could tell my brother respected me for getting out of bed so early each day, just because I wanted to help him. I could tell he valued my companionship – even though he was 10 ½ years old, being on the street alone so early in the morning is not a nice place to be. I am sure he welcomed the company.

That paper-route time I shared with my brother bonded us for life. We were always close after that. Later we ended up sharing a room when our father converted that unfinished attic into three bedrooms. With ten kids in the family, he had to fit us in wherever he could.

I'll never forget the day Jim left for the Army after being drafted. With the Vietnam War in full swing, I was afraid we might never see each other again. When my brother said goodbye that morning, I cried. I would miss him so much.

My eyes were swollen and red when I left the house that day for high school. I didn't want to admit to crying, so I told my friends who asked about my red eyes that I just had a bad cold.

I thought of him often that day. I prayed and I told God that I'd be good if He let my brother come home safe. Little did I know that Jim would be back at the house even before I got home. It seems that when he went for the induction physical, he was rejected because of a bad knee. Jim was only in the Army for a few hours and he never went to Vietnam.

I often reflect on that day and how excited I was to walk into the house and see my brother sitting there.

I can't put into words how thankful I was then, and how thankful I am today for the leadership he showed me over the years. Jim became my protector, whether defending me from a bully on the street, standing up to a neighbor kid who stole my football, or stepping in for me with my parents when there was something he thought I needed.

Receiving my
own first bike

"Finally something to call mine."

Along with the brotherly bond that lasted a life time, Jim also gave me a very special gift for all those mornings getting up at 5:00 a.m. to help him on his paper route. It wasn't something I expected and was never part of the "helping on the paper route deal," but that's part of what made it a great gift.

Jim and I never discussed pay, nor did I expect any. But one spring, he used his own money to buy me a bicycle. I can still see it: a 20-inch Schwinn, green and white paint with Bendix brakes. By today's standards, it might not have been much of a bike, but to this day it remains one of the best gifts I ever received.

Despite receiving that gift more than 60 years ago, I remember the day as if it were yesterday. I loved that green Schwinn and the feeling I had when I rode it. That bike was one of my most prized possessions.

The bike did cause a major family incident, however. With ten kids, there was a kind of hierarchy and everything was *supposed* to be done in age order. With Jim's gift, I became the proud owner of a bicycle *before* my older brother Ed (rest in peace) got one. It caused a big stink in the family. Jim stuck to his guns and insisted it was his decision on how to spend his own money – and he had decided to buy me a bike for all the help I was giving him.

There was only one problem, which was major: since I'd never had a bike before, I had no idea how to ride one. I was determined to learn, though. I threw some training wheels on there and in the span of one day, I went from training wheels to riding without them. Yep, all in one day. My mom didn't like that I had ruined a pair of jeans and had given myself two bloody knees during my riding lessons. But I proved myself an accomplished bicyclist in just a few hours.

I loved that bike (I know, I said it before). I washed it every day, and sometimes twice a day. It's funny how something like being given a bike ended up having such a major impact in my life. But life was so simple back then, so maybe it didn't take much at the age of five.

That paper route and the unexpected gift of a bicycle taught me the value of helping others and expecting nothing in return. It made me feel like even though I was a little kid, I could pitch in and help, and that I did have value. Knocking out training wheels in one day was an early lesson that showed me that when I really want to accomplish something, I can do it.

Some kids
blossom late

"I'm sorry, you have not passed the entrance exam to enter this high school."

My oldest brother Jim struggled as a student in grade school. Part of his struggle might have been due to him being heavyset. By eighth grade, I think he was about 5 foot 9 inches tall, and well over 200 lbs. While other school kids might have made fun of Jim for his size, my brothers and sisters and I looked up to him as our oldest brother and leader.

Among our Irish Catholic community on Chicago's South Side, there was an expectation to attend one of the several Catholic high schools in the area, and our family strove to live up to those expectations. Jim ran into trouble when didn't pass the entrance exams for any of these local Catholic high schools. It looked like my brother might be headed to a public high school.

You could get a fine education at a public high school, but as Catholics, we felt an obligation to our faith to attend one of the Catholic schools. From one school after another, Jim heard a variation on: "Sorry, you didn't pass our entrance exam." Just when it appeared all was lost, my parents heard about a new Catholic high school that had just opened. Lucky for Jim, they needed to bring in new students, so there was no entrance exam. It might not have been the most ideal academic decision, but at least it was an opportunity for Jim to meet our Catholic obligation by attending a Catholic school.

A funny thing happened, though, during the four years that Jim attended that high school. He ended up on the honor roll the last three years, graduated with honors, and also won an award as the top accounting student in his class. Here was a guy who four years prior could not pass an entrance exam, and he was now excelling in his classes. In addition, his weight problem went away as his frame filled out. Jim graduated from high school at 6 foot 4, and a solid 225 lbs.

I was the fifth of ten kids, and like most of my siblings, we followed in Jim's footsteps and ended up attending that same high school. The school turned out to be a great match for our family, and we were a great match for the school. This is just one of the many examples where I could see how the Universe showed up with answer or opportunity, even if it wasn't the one we expected.

My late-blooming brother Jim went on to a successful business career, and obtained his master's degree from a prestigious university that has one of the most difficult entrance requirements in the nation. By his example, Jim showed me that I should never give up, and that I should hold onto hope while the Universe gets around to showing up with help.

Jim set an example of how some people simply blossom late. Over the years, I've watched people grow, and I always reach back and remind myself of Jim's example of how people bloom at different times. Watching Jim's experiences taught me to never let anyone pigeonhole me into a category, and for me to never put a label like "slow" or "failure" on another person. They may just be a late bloomer.

Embarrassment can drive you to work harder

"What people think of me is none of my business."

My father had medical issues at the age of 48. He was a self-employed plumber who worked many hours. Until his illness, he was a great provider and we never lacked for anything. Once he got sick, he was forced to cut back on his working hours and eventually had to retire. This change in his employment affected our family income dramatically. My mother had to get creative to figure out how to keep twelve people fed and clothed. It was not easy. For the most part, we lived from paycheck-to-paycheck after his illness.

I'm not complaining. I'm very happy with my childhood experiences and I wouldn't change a single thing about it. Those experiences made me who I am today and I am happy with that. Nevertheless, money was tight and seldom did we get anything new. My clothes were usually hand-me-downs from my older brothers.

While it was unusual for any *one* of us to get something new, it was almost *impossible* for *all* of us to get anything new – all at the same time. But one Easter, my mother showed us that nothing was impossible. My mother's devotion to our family was very strong; she was proud of each and every one of us. We could all tell by the way she looked at us – she left no doubt that she loved us.

She had that look on her face when she went out and bought us all brand-new parkas (called hoodies today) for Easter. I can still see the pride in her face, and her big smile of accomplishment. She was so excited to have us all wear our new parkas to Easter Mass, and my brothers could tell this was a special occasion, too. This had never happened before... all of us having something new to wear all at the same time.

That excitement didn't last long, however. For us boys, most of our peers at Easter Mass were wearing shirts and ties. While we looked good in our new parkas, we also looked out of place. It didn't take long for our peers to start making comments about the way we looked. I can't say their criticism didn't bother me at all, but I'm glad to say it didn't bother me as much as they wanted it to. Any embarrassment we felt was far outweighed by our pride in our new parkas and our gratitude to our mother for making sacrifices in other areas to make it happen.

I admit to feeling embarrassed by the teasing from the other kids, but I learned something important at the same time: what other people think of me is none of my business. Even more, the experience showed me what could happen when you were willing to work harder. I could see how hard my mother and father worked just to make ends meet, but we were import-ant enough for to them to buy all "the boys" warm parkas all at once.

Their example of hard work drove us all to work harder. I know it drove me. While we may not have had all the material things that other families had, we were grateful for whatever was given to us – and we knew that hard work was the way to get the things we needed.

The Easter Mass/Embarrassing Parka Incident took place over 60 years ago. But even after these six decades, I've never forgotten the pride on my mother's face as we all donned our new coats. No teasing in the world could take that feeling away from us.

I was an 18-year-old know-it-all

"Son, your adult life starts today. And you are not ready!"

I graduated from high school in June of 1968. Graduation day had been pinned on my calendar for years, and I couldn't wait to go out and take on the world. I admit to having a poor academic record in high school, though. Back then, a college degree was not the major requirement it is today, so going to college was not on my to-do list. I had myself a part-time job at an electrical supply store, and they had promised me full-time work when I graduated. I was ready.

The day of my graduation party, the house was full of excitement and everyone was helping to get ready. I had to get something from my parent's room. When I went in, I saw my father sitting on the side of the bed with that "concerned dad" look on his face. I asked him if there was something wrong. He said, "Son, your adult life starts today. And you are not ready!"

I disagreed. "I'm *more* than ready, Dad, and I've been ready for a long time," I claimed. "There's no need to worry about me."

Little did I know that my dad would turn out to be right. He saw me for the young immature guy I was, someone who had to grow before he could call himself an adult. Unfortunately, it took me a long time to grow up and I made a ton of mistakes before I eventually became the mature adult I had *supposed* myself to be back in 1968.

What my dad saw in me then was a kid who thought he knew it all, and who wasn't yet teachable. To be teachable, one must be humble – and I was *not* humble at all. If I had listened to my dad back then, I would have spent more time on the books, studying, and planning for my long-range future – and less time planning this weekend's party. At age 18, all I wanted to do was hang out with friends and stay out late. My dad was a family man, and family always came first. If there was something I could change, I would have listened earlier about the importance of family. I thought there'd always be time for that later.

My dad passed away in 1970 when I was only 20. I was just two years out of high school and still thought I knew everything. If I could change anything looking back, I'd want more time with my dad. I would have opened myself earlier to take more of his fatherly advice to heart. My dad passed away long before my mature lights came on, so he never got to know me as the mature man I became. But maybe he does know the man I've become. I believe in my core that our loved ones who pass on, they still keep an eye on us. I know Dad has gotten me out of a lot of scrapes along the way.

I'm not saying I would change anything about the past, because where I am today is right where I need to be. If I were to change something in the past, that might change the person I am now. We can't look back with regret. We have to live out our own stories and make our own decisions, and sometimes that means we miss out on the wisdom of older people. Being a young know-it-all, I know that I often missed out on many of those messages of advice.

As I've gotten older, I'm better able to see how life goes by so quickly. I've learned to savor each day with my family. I've found the value in paying particular attention to older people, who have wisdom you can use. I've learned it's better to not wait to tell people how you feel about them – tell them now.

I didn't have a sense of this wisdom when I was age 18 or age 20, and I never got the opportunity to really thank my dad for all he did for me and my siblings. It was years before I could see in hindsight how well my dad knew me on that nice spring day back in June 1968, when he told me I wasn't yet ready.

My brother who was born old

"What are your plans for the future?"

In the 1940s when my dad and mom got married, most people were tying the knot in their early 20s. On their wedding day, my mom was 27 and my father was 32 – so you might say they "got married later in life." With their peers having a head start on them, my parents wasted no time in starting our family. Between 1944 and 1959, they brought ten of us into this world: eight boys and two girls. I was the fifth child and fifth boy to come along: one boy a year for the first five years. Can you imagine a house with five boys under the age of six? While none of us were born in the same year, we came in quick order: Jim (RIP) was born in November of 1944, Dennis in June 1946, John in July of 1947, Ed (RIP) in November 1948, and me in May of 1950.

My oldest brother Jim was exactly 5 ½ years older than me (to the day). Despite being a few years older, Jim was light years ahead of me in maturity. He seemed like he was born old. As we grew up and my parents added five more children to the family, it was a challenge for my parents to keep track of us all. My dad was busy working and making money to support the dozen of us in the family. My mom worked full-time at home, keeping us children fed and in clean clothes. She did head back into the work force when my youngest brother was less than a year old. My father got sick in 1958 and eventually had to stop working all together.

Where my dad and mom may have been too busy keep up the household, my brother Jim took on a kind of parenting role for me. He took me under his wing. Jim was always looking out for me, showing me lessons, offering advice, and making sure I had what I needed. Jim bought me my first bike. He also bought me my first shotgun, and we hunted together each winter. Jim even got me a part-time job in an electrical supply store while I was in high school.

When I graduated from high school in 1968, I didn't have ambitions to attend college. I wasn't what you'd call a scholar, and with my attitude and an admitted lack of maturity, I didn't see college in my future. Plus, I had work lined up for after high school. The electrical supply store where I worked part-time had offered me a full-time job, so I felt like I was all set up to start on my adult life. I didn't put much thought into the idea that working in a family-owned electrical supply store did not have much room to grow and prosper.

One summer evening after graduation, I was having some dinner in the kitchen with Jim. He asked me, "So, what are your plans for the future?"

"Let me see," I responded. "There's a party this Friday night and another one on Saturday."

Jim said, "I'm not talking about weekend plans, Larry. I'm talking your future plans"

"I don't know," I said. "This weekend is about as far as I've planned out so far."

My oldest brother Jim then did something that changed the course of my life. He told me that the place where he worked was looking to hire someone to train as a computer operator. Jim said there was a future in computers (remember that this was 1968). He said he felt I would be good at it, and said he thought he could help get me a job there.

I told Jim I would try it for a while and see how it goes. I started that trainee job on September 9, 1968. That one job led to a future for myself and the family I would come to raise. That little trainee job led to a 45-year career in the computer industry, which provided for my wife and family and put our four children through college.

I've learned that people in your life can sometimes have a better understanding of you than you have of yourself. They have a kind of wisdom. Some people are just born old, and my oldest brother Jim was one of those people. Jim passed away when he was only 60 years old. In our years together as brothers, he showed that he understood me, and he helped me understand myself. Jim left behind a wealth of wisdom and a legacy of warm memories of our time together. I was blessed to have him in my life.

While Jim helped guide me in my early years, when my father died when I was age 20, Jim and my brothers Dennis, John, and Ed really stepped up as leaders of our house. All of them kept an eye on me.

Setting a goal and planning your steps to get there

"Checks need to be in the mailroom by 4:00 p.m." My first information technology job was on second shift and I worked from 4:00 p.m. to midnight. That's where I started to learn the business. After about nine months on second shift, I was offered a job on first shift, working from 8:00 a.m. to 4:00 p.m. I jumped at the chance to work "normal" hours.

The responsibilities on day shift were much the same as evening shift, with a couple important exceptions. For example, first shift had the task of running processes that resulted in the printing of payment checks that went out to our providers. Some of these customers were government providers, which would apply a penalty if we did not complete the processing and deliver the checks to the mail room by 4:00 p.m. each day. It was an aggressive goal, but it was not impossible.

25

When I went to first shift, however, I found that we almost never met the 4:00 p.m. mail-room deadline. I found that processing was completed and checks were delivered the mail room on time maybe once every 15 days.

I was not in a management role yet, but I set a personal goal to work hard and take the initiative to improve on the success rate of meeting this daily deadline. I shared my ideas with my new manager. He liked my ideas, and said, "I'll make you a deal. Each day you make checks on time, I'll buy you a cup of coffee."

At the time, coffee was 10 cents in the cafeteria. So with that huge financial incentive in mind, I set about to improve our processing efficiency to get those checks to the mail room by the 4:00 p.m. deadline. Things started out a little slow, but eventually we got into a good flow and we started meeting that daily deadline. Some of the changes I made included adjusting schedules and identifying some process that could run concurrently. I instituted regular maintenance and cleaning of the equipment, which reduced errors in processing. In my own schedule, I was able to adjust my breaks and lunch hour around long-running jobs so there was no interruption to the process. Things got better. In fact, we improved so much that we were recognized for meeting the deadline for 60 days in a row.

I don't feel like I did anything unusual, and others could have done the same. The difference was that I simply focused on the details, executed a plan, and did not accept the excuse that the goal of checks at 4 p.m. is next to impossible. Often times we are told that something "can't be done." Don't buy into all you hear, and challenge yourself to be a leader.

Offering sincere compliments, and being willing to receive them

"You are going to make a great father."

Over the course of my 45 years in business, I've had many thousands of conversations with people from every walk of life. I've reflected how some of those conversations affected me so much that, even though the conversation happened decades ago, they still rise up in my mind and bring a happy feeling. One of those conversations happened way back in 1970 when I was working in the information technology (IT) shop for an insurance company.

Each morning a particular customer of mine would come to pick up reports that we'd processed the prior evening. Each morning, she and I would exchange pleasantries – maybe something about the weather or stories appearing in the current news. One particular morning, we had a conversation that I've never forgotten. I was 19 and single at the time. I'd guess my customer must have been about 40 at the time, and single also. Our conversation somehow turned to the topic of raising children. Coming from a family of 12, with eight brothers and two sisters, I had some practical experience in what raising children looked like. I shared some stories about how supportive my father was to each of his children. I always knew my dad was in my corner and learned from him how important it is for a parent to be supportive of their children. I always knew home was safe zone the minute I walked in our front door.

We talked and each shared our ideas on the right way to raise children. At one point in the conversation, my customer looked me right in the eye and she said, "I think you are going to make a great father."

Her words surprised me. While my thoughts and comments about parenting were based on my experience growing up in a big family, any ideas of me as "a father" were hypothetical. I had no family plans at the time, and in fact was not even dating anyone seriously, much less thinking of myself as a father.

While her compliment took me aback, at the same time they made me feel really good about the person I was. Her simple comment set a stage for me, and had me setting an expectation for myself. I knew from that point on that I could live up to "being a great father." Over the years that would follow, meeting my wife and raising own children, that simple sentence has entered my mind many times. I made some mistakes along the way, like we all do as parents. But I often found myself recalling her words, which became like an anthem to me: "You're going to make a great father." It reminded me to focus on doing those things I knew a great father would do.

My mother use to always tell me, "If you don't have anything good to say about someone, don't say anything at all." While I understand that message, there is also a lesson in giving people positive feedback. I have a hunch that customer of mine (whose name I don't even recall now) does not recall that conversation from nearly 50 years ago, but I remember it like it was yesterday. I might not remember a conversations I had yesterday morning, but the "great father" conversation with her is always fresh in my mind.

I found over the years that people sometimes tend to minimize their own accomplishments. I make sure that, when it is deserved, I'll tell a clerk in a store that I think they're doing a good job. I'll tell a cashier at a fast food restaurant that I appreciate the good service. There's always and opportunity to give a compliment. Make sure you use those opportunities.

Life can come at you quicker than you expect

"I am due in April!"

My wife Debbie and I met when we were working at the same company. She was 18 and I was 19. I remember seeing her one day in the company cafeteria. She was (and still is) extremely good looking. Even standing in line in the cafeteria her blonde hair and bright smile swept me off my feet. She took my breath away. To say I was swept away is an understatement. From the first time I saw her, I knew this was someone I needed to meet. I was in love.

As we got our food in the cafeteria that day, I remember saying to a buddy I was going to lunch with that I'd really like to meet her. As we got into the checkout line, she happened to be right in front of us. Knowing I was shy at age 19, my buddy took matters into his own hands. He tapped her on the shoulder. "This guy here," he said, pointing to me, "wants to meet you." I probably turned fifty shades of red.

She looked past my buddy to me and said, "If he wants to meet me, then why doesn't he?"

As we talked, she told me that she was engaged at the time. So, I respected that engagement ring and moved on. As luck would have it though, I soon found out that her fiancé was overseas and that she planned to break up with him. Thinking I might have a chance, I got up the nerve to talk to her again and invited her to the bowling alley where the company league played on Thursday nights. Big-time romance guy, right?

Much to my surprise, she showed up. We chatted that night, seemed to hit it off, and by Christmas, we were steady dating. We spent a lot of time together those first six months. If I thought her outsides were beautiful when we first met, I found an equivalent inner beauty the more time we spent together. We were a typical carefree young couple of the early 1970's and clueless of what our futures might bring. Life was one big party.

As we got more serious, we started discussing marriage. Our wedding plans got accelerated, though, when she told me one evening in mid-August: "I'm 'due' in April!"

For a couple as young as we were, this news was quite a shock. But I am a firm believer that nothing happens by accident, and I believe that this unplanned baby was no exception. Debbie and I discussed our options. We agreed we should move up our wedding plans, and get married as soon as possible. We were married in October. Six months later, our son Larry Jr. was born.

Were we ready? Nope. We were young and we took chances we never should have. But we decided together to share our lives, with all the surprises that would come. Debbie and I pushed ahead with our lives, and learned together along the way. We've had our share of bumps and scrapes along this journey, but we have survived all of those and we've grown closer together each year. Making a marriage work takes compromise, being willing to adjust, and putting a priority on mutual understanding.

So many times, I hear songs that remind me of when we met and the life we were building together. Kenny Chesney's "You Had Me From Hello" or Shania Twain's "You're Still the One" or Randy Travis's "For-ever and Ever, Amen." The song that really comes to mind is "Good Hearted Women" by Waylon Jennings and Willie Nelson.

"Good Hearted Woman" became one of "our songs" the year my wife Debbie and I were at the Illinois State Fair, attending a Willie Nelson concert with my cousin Sharon. When Willie started singing this song, Sharon turned to Debbie and said, "Many people in the family think of you every time we hear this song." I sat there and listened to the words and wondered, "What do they mean by that?" It was much later I figured out what my cousin meant, with song lyrics like:

She's a good-hearted woman in love with a good-timin' man

She loves him in spite of his ways that she don't understand

Through teardrops and laughter, they'll pass through this world hand-in-hand,

A good-hearted woman loving her good timing man

Looking back, I'm glad we made the right decision to be together. And 48 years later, here we are: together, and blessed with three additional daughters and 14 grandchildren.

On this journey of family, I've come to understand "love" as a verb, not as noun. Love is the action of caring for those around you, adjusting for things that are important to them, and appreciating them for who they are, regardless of our expectations of them. Love can sometimes be difficult, but we've stuck with it, worked together to move through the issues, and have only gotten closer as the years have rolled on.

Empowered by my
first manager

"I heard you are going back to your old job."
I was 24 years old and moving up in the IT shop at the company where I worked. Even though I was performing well, however, I got passed over for a promotion and felt it was time to look for something where my skills would be recognized. I found a new job as an IT shift manager for another company. My new manager Ken recognized my management capabilities and potential. In my new role, he said he needed me to take charge and show the other shift managers how to keep things running smoothly. He told me the lead shift manager position was mine for the taking.

For the first couple months, things seemed to be going okay in the new role, but I didn't feel like I was being given the opportunities to lead and help the others, as my boss had promised. About two months into this new job, my old company called. They told me they wanted me back and made me a pretty good offer.

Since things were not going as planned in my new job, I was seriously considering going back to my old company. I let slip to some of my coworkers that I was probably going to leave. Naturally, the news got back to my new boss. Ken came into my office one day and said he wanted to talk. I figured he'd found out about my plans to leave, and would probably try to convince me to stay, just like others had in the past. I got a surprise.

"I heard you're planning to go back to your old company," Ken said.

"That's right," I said.

"Help me out here," he said, "and help me understand what went wrong. When I interviewed you and asked why you wanted to leave your old job, you said you'd been passed over for a promotion. That you were looking for a new challenge. Is that correct?"

I agreed. He asked me what had changed.

I told him my biggest issue was when I was hired, he told me he wanted me to take charge and be the lead shift manager, and that was not happening.

Ken said, "Now I'm really confused. What do you mean it's not happening?" But then he paused and said, "Oh, I got it. You're looking to *me* to do those things *for you*. If that's the case, then by all means you should go back to your old company. If I have to take charge and lead *for you*, then I don't need you. But I still feel you're a great fit here, and could do well. But the *doing* is your responsibility, not mine. My offer to support you *as you take charge* still stands."

My experience in the past had been that if I wanted anything on the job, I would go to management – and they would either give me what I needed, or help me get it. Not this time, though. Ken was challenging me to take the reins and act on my own, with him supporting me but not doing it for me. For the first time in my short professional career, I felt both challenged and empowered.

I made my first empowered decision: I turned down the offer from the old company and stayed working with Ken for another 13 years. He was a major mentor in my life and taught me so much about life. Although I left that company over 30 years ago, Ken and I are still friends. What made our friendship more special was that Ken is African American. In the early 1970s, working in a southern-based company, it wasn't typical for a white Irish guy from the Southside of Chicago and an African American guy to be buddies.

Ken and I spent many hours together over those 13 years, both on the job and socially outside the job. He shared a lot of wisdom with me, not only work related but just how to be a better man.

Ken was the first manager who truly empowered me. He taught me how to take responsibility, to manage, and to empower other people – not doing the work for them, but giving them the authority and responsibility to figure out problems for themselves. I owe him much for letting me stand on my own two feet.

Because of Ken's influence, I was able to mentor others, as well. I was able to bring Ken's influence into my personal life, by using his lessons to empower my children – telling them I believed in them, but not doing their work for them. Ken's impact on my life has even carried forward with our grandchildren, as I encourage them the way Ken encouraged me.

Cheaper doesn't mean better

"Why are you selling these puppies for only $150?"

Our family was young. Debbie and I had two small children and very little money. For some reason, this seemed like the perfect time to spend a couple hundred to buy an Afghan hound. To be fair, my wife had always dreamed of owning a long-haired Afghan. So despite being financially strapped, I started on my dog search.

I wanted a good quality dog, so I set my minimum price at $225. I focused my search on female Afghans – I figured with a female, we could breed her, have a litter, and recover the cost. After a bit of searching, I found a female Afghan with good pedigree and within our price range. I made the purchase and surprised my wife with a new Afghan puppy we named Shilo.

With two small children in a small two-bedroom house, raising an Afghan puppy was not easy. Afghans are known for their looks, not for their brains. Shilo was not very disciplined and took a lot of time and attention to properly train, but we loved her. We raised her and got her to the age where she was old enough to breed.

During my walks in the neighborhood, I ran into a neighbor who was walking two male Afghans, one dog the sire and the other, his son. We got to talking and the neighbor said he would be definitely be interested in mating our dogs. We agreed on his price: he would get the pick of the litter.

After checking with our veterinarian, we determined when would be the right time to breed Shilo and the "date" was set. On the appointed day, I took Shilo over to the neighbor's house. She was playing hard-to-get and wanted nothing to do with either of the male Afghans. Like the "young bull, old bull" story, the young dog was overly eager, ready and rushing. The older hound was gentler and more patient, and eventually was the one who mated with Shilo.

After a few weeks, our vet confirmed it: we now had a pregnant Afghan hound to add to an already busy household. Our bungalow was small, but we had a "walk-in" pantry that we decided would be the perfect size for a dog nursery. When the day came, my wife and young son daughter (age four and one at the time) and I all welcomed eight healthy Afghan hound puppies into our fold.

It was most amazing to observe the change in Shilo's behavior. She had previously been an out-of-control, no-discipline, hard-to-train dog. But with the arrival of her eight puppies, she showed herself as an incredible mother, seemed to know exactly what to do, and took care of those puppies more than I ever thought her capable of. Although Shilo had always been a friendly and outgoing dog, after her pups were born, she would tolerate no strangers in the house. Our family were the only ones she'd allow near her pups.

As the puppies grew, Christmas was approaching. The puppies would turn six weeks old a few weeks before Christmas. The timing was perfect. I figured if I priced them right, I could place the weaned pups with their new owners just in time for Yuletide.

Our busy lives got even busier as we prepared for Christmas in a home with two small children and seven rapidly growing puppies (the breeder had taken his pick of the litter). As the puppies get older and were weaned, Shilo was not feeding them anymore, so making sure they were fed became our responsibility. Shilo never was much for cleaning up after them, so that job always fell to us. To keep the pantry/dog nursery from getting destroyed, we cleaned it out at least twice a day.

As Christmas approached, I put an ad in the paper to find homes for the remaining seven puppies. I priced them low, hoping that would help us sell them quickly:

"Afghan Hound Pups. Four females and three males. Full pedigreed. $150 each."

I figured that in a few short days, we would find new homes for the Afghan pups, have an extra thousand dollars for Christmas, and have the pantry and our lives back to normal. But five days passed and we received not one single call. The feedings and puppy clean-ups continued.

Finally, I got a call from a woman who asked if she could come and see the pups, and asked if she could bring her veterinarian along with her. I said sure, so they came over. They looked at the pups and really liked "Maude" (yes, my wife and children had named all of the puppies; if it were up to them, we probably would have kept them all). The woman and her vet had a private conversation in another room. They must have liked what they saw, because she came back and gave me a check for $150 and walked out the door with Maude (more on this transaction in a moment). We were finally on our way: one puppy down and six more to go.

But another week went by, and the phone wasn't ringing. The pups continued to gobble the puppy-chow. As they grew, their "output" grew, too. Finally on a Sunday afternoon, I got a call from a guy who was interested. He asked if he could come and

see the pups, and also wanted to see the mother. I
told him to come on over. I let him know he could
see Shilo, but he'd have to view her from a house
window – whenever visitors came, we had to put
her in the yard because she wouldn't let non-family
members into the house.

The fellow arrived with three of his children in tow.
He told me they had owned an Afghan hound as their
family pet, and that she died suddenly that week. The
man and his children looked our puppies over, and
loved what they saw. His next comment has changed
my life and my view of how to value and price things.

"Why are you selling these puppies for only $150?
These puppies are worth $300 each," he said.

"When I saw your ad, I almost passed you by. I
figured that something must be wrong with this litter
if the pups are only $150 each. This is the sixth litter
of Afghans we've looked at today," he said. "Honestly,
these are by far the best puppies of them all."

They fell in love with one of the pups, and the man
offered to pay $300 for it. I told him, "I advertised
these puppies for $150, so how about you just pay me
the $150." The man gave me a check for $150, but not
before making me promise that I would change the ad
and price these Afghan pups at $300.

I took his suggestion and changed the ad the next
day from $150 to $300. Would you believe that we sold
all the remaining five puppies the very next day?

People look for value, and often base that perceived value on the price. I reminded myself that when I purchased Shilo, I had started looking at $225. But when I underpriced her pups at $150, nobody called. Once I raised the perceived value of the puppies, people didn't blink at paying $300. Making the price of something cheaper does not always make it easier to sell.

I have used this lesson many times since those puppy days. I also learned that while a low price might get someone interested, a low price could also get you eliminated before even being in the game.

I learned another valuable lesson in the transaction where we sold Maude for $150. The woman who was buying Maude brought her veterinarian with her. They were surely aware that these puppies were underpriced, but never felt the need to share that with us. Adding to the complications, with all the chaos of Christmas upon us, we somehow lost the $150 check. I called the woman and explained my dilemma. I asked if she would be willing to resend another check. I even suggested that she stop payment on the lost check, take that out of the total, and just send me a check for $140. She said she would, but her payment never arrived. All of my calls after that were ignored. At the time, there was no voicemail, email, Facebook, Twitter, or any of the other ways we have to contact each other today. I'm talking old school. I chalked it up as a loss.

However, a year later at the following Christmas, I was taking ornaments out of a Christmas box and guess what I found? That lost $150 check. I guessed that one of the children might have put it in there the year before. I went right to the bank to cash the check, and it cleared. The buyer apparently hadn't wanted to spend the $10 to protect herself. I'm sure that seeing her check clear a year later was a surprise to her. Always be honest.

Expectations are everything

"They always win."

When my son Larry was in second grade, I had the opportunity to help my landlord, who was coaching his son's baseball team. Larry was too young to play in the league, but I knew he'd soon be old enough. When he was old enough to start playing, I wanted to be his coach – and getting some early coaching experience sounded like a good idea.

Our team consisted of third, fourth, and fifth grade boys from the local Catholic grammar school. This league had been around for years. The kids really looked forward to competing against their friends and peers. Team rosters were, for the most part, the luck of the draw. Names were picked, we formed our teams, and we started our practices. I was having a good time getting to know these kids. As we started to practice, I could tell that they had skills and that we had a pretty good team.

With the start of the season only a few days away, we had one more practice before the first game. When

I showed up for our last practice before opening day, I could see that the kids looked dejected. They were definitely not as excited as I had seen them at our previous practices. I asked what was going on. They told me that the schedule had been posted at school and our first game was against Mr. Daly's team.

They told me that Mr. Daly had been coaching in the baseball league for years. His teams were often formidable. To quote one of the kids on my team: "Mr. Daly's teams always win the league."

I thought about what the kids were telling me. I considered that our team had never seen Mr. Daly's team practice, and many had no idea who was even on Mr. Daly's team. But because of rumor and myth and expectations, my team already felt like they didn't have a chance. How could they be beaten before they even started?

I gathered the kids together. I told them that based on what I'd seen from all our practices, they were a really good team, and it would take a very good Daly team to beat us. I'm not sure how much the kids believed me at the time. But the encouragement started to put a little grain of doubt into their theory that "Mr. Daly's team always wins."

"All you have to do is show up ready to play your best," I told the team. "We'll make sure we make Daly's team play *their* best, too. And from there, we'll just see what happens." Again, I'm not sure they believed, but

I think *they* bought into *my* belief that they might be able to win.

Opening day arrived and we found ourselves in a close and hard-fought game. As the innings ticked by, and we stayed in the game. The kids started to see that they *were* competitive with Mr. Daly's team. Our kids started to believe that maybe we *could* win.

We went into the bottom of the ninth inning, and found ourselves leading Mr. Daly's team by a score of 7 to 4. With one out and the bases empty, Daly's big slugger came up to the plate. He smacked a solid home run, which made the score 7 to 5. I looked at our kids on the field, and I could see by their body language that they were thinking, "Here we go. I *knew* we would lose."

We were playing well and ahead by two runs, and only need to get two more outs to win the game. I called a time-out and gathered the team on the mound. I reminded them that they only needed two more outs. Get those two outs and they would be the best team in the league. "Hold your heads high," I said. "Nobody thought we had a chance, but here we are – in this game and two outs away from winning it."

I could see their moods change. They seemed energized and seem to stand straighter. It *was* possible. Maybe we *can* beat the best team in the league. The next two batters came to plate. Two up and two down, and we found that we'd won the game. If our team was shocked by our victory, Mr. Daly's team seemed to be in even greater shock – they weren't used to losing.

It wasn't just that game, either. Because we had taken charge of our expectations and found that we *could* win against the best team in the league, we never lost a game that season.

Expectations are not always based on fact. If you can change your expectations just a little, you'd be surprised at what good things can happen.

Politeness pays
dividends

"Good morning. This is Betty. How can I help you today?"

At one point in my career, the company where I worked had a reduction in forces. In the reorganization that followed, I was assigned to manage a staff of telephone operators, even though I had absolutely no experience in that type of work. Adding to the challenges, these were union positions, and these switchboard-operator roles were often the last stop for employees before being let out the door. The attitude and morale among the operators left a lot to be desired.

As I went about familiarizing myself with the work of my new team, I found it was the common practice for the operators to answer every call in the following manner:

"XYZ Company"

That was it. No "Hello." No "This is Larry." Just the curt, low-morale voice of an unidentified employee who said nothing more than, "XYZ Company." (That's not the actual name, but the company did go by only three letters.)

You can imagine the poor first impression made on every person who called our switchboard. Whether that caller be a potential customer, a vendor, a family member, or the press, I can tell you that this kind of clipped greeting was definitely making a poor first impression. To compound the problem, when callers received such an unfriendly greeting from the operators, callers often returned the favor by replying with the same kind of surly attitude.

To help me understand my people and their work better, I had started reading a book about customer service. I found a story in there about the customer service practices of a successful phone company. They discovered that when operators answering the phone did a simple thing like saying their names, customer satisfaction improved dramatically. The study showed that when callers heard an operator sharing their name on the other end of the line, the callers seemed to relax and be in a better mood.

I reflected on my personal experience with this kind of good customer service. I could recall several times I had issues with my phone company, perhaps billing or ordering errors. I'd punch in the numbers to make my call, upset over being inconvenienced and ready to go after someone. But a funny thing happened when the operator on the other end answered: "Good morning, this is Melissa with Bell Corporation. How can I help you?"

With that greeting of "good morning," the person sharing their name, and their offer to be helpful, my irritation seemed to melt away. I was able to relax and to realize "Melissa" on the other end of the phone was a person with a job to do, and not someone who was personally responsible for the error on my phone bill. With this first-hand experience and the supporting examples from the customer-service book, I decided to try and apply some of these practices with the operator crew I just was assigned to manage.

The switchboard group supervisor was named Betty. She had been a supervisor for many years, and I am sure she was not interested in hearing any bright ideas from a young guy who had no switchboard experience at all. I sat down with Betty and I said, "I realize I don't have the experience you have and I've never been a phone operator, but I do have a couple suggestions that I think might help you and the company."

Betty crossed her arms and looked at me with an expression I interpreted as: "Oh boy, here comes some stupid idea." I continued, "I'd like you and the other operators to try something new when you answer the phones. I'd like you to answer incoming calls as: "XYZ

Corporation. This is Betty speaking. How may I help you today?"

Betty gave me a skeptical smirk and said, "Mr. Walsh, with all due respect, that will never work. We just don't have the time to answer the phones with all that." I said, "I understand, and I admit that I don't know what it's like to do your job. But I'll ask you and the other operators to please try this for one week. If after a week, it's just not working, we can go back to the old way." Betty said, "Okay. But it's not going to work." She got up and walked out of the meeting.

A few days later, Betty came into my office, closed the door, and sat down. She had a sheepish smile on her face, and I got the feeling she was a much happier person than the one who was in my office just a few days prior. She said, "Mr. Walsh, I owe you a big apology. Your suggestion is working great. My operators are telling me that callers are responding well to the longer, friendlier greeting. Many of them saying things like, 'Oh, it's so nice to hear a name to go along with the voice.' They're much more pleasant to speak with compared to the way we were answering the phones before. Honestly, I have never enjoyed my job more than I have these past few days."

Based on Betty's feedback, it was clear that the friendly operator greeting was working even better than I had hoped. I expected that callers would have a more positive customer experience, but I didn't realize that our operators would also benefit so much and enjoy their workdays so much more. Looking back now, it makes sense.

From these practical examples, I could see how much one's helpful tone of voice and use of respectful, courteous greetings can improve the quality of an interaction with other people. The better you treat people, the better you will be treated. Sometimes, simple courtesies like that can make another person's day, and can make you feel better about your day, as well. It might not always work... you may run into someone who takes advantage of you, or doesn't respond to the courtesy, but that's on them. You only have to worry about what you are doing and how you treat other people.

Appreciating the influence teachers have in our lives

"Your name isn't Mandy... it's Amanda!"
"Amanda is the third of your children I've had in my class. She seems a little behind where her brother and sister were at this stage." This is the message my wife Debbie and I heard at our first parent-teacher conference with Amanda's kindergarten teacher. It would be an understatement to say this comment set us aback. As my wife and I walked home in a daze, we talked about what might be going wrong.

With a little questioning, we discovered that Amanda and this teacher had got off on the wrong foot from day one. On the first day of kindergarten, the teacher took roll call. When she asked if "Amanda Walsh" was present, my daughter just sat there. We had always called her "Mandy," which was the only name she knew. When the teacher paged "Amanda Walsh," our daughter had no idea who that was.

Amanda shared with us how the teacher had embarrassed her in class. When Amanda didn't respond to the constant page, this teacher found it necessary to get in her face and say loudly, "*Amanda Walsh!*" My daughter responded calmly, "I am *Mandy* Walsh." The kindergarten teacher tried to inform her that "Her Proper Name" was *Amanda* Walsh.

Even at the age of five, Amanda had always been an independent person. When this teacher embarrassed her in front of the class, she quite frankly did not like the teacher from that point on. I got the feeling this kindergarten teacher didn't much like Amanda, either. It's sad to think that when a teacher can have so much influence on a young child, the teacher would choose to intimidate a child, when the teacher is supposed to be the responsible adult.

Amanda survived kindergarten and moved on to first grade. What a difference a year makes, or I should I say, "What a difference a teacher makes." Amanda's first-grade teacher was named Ms. Rasiniack. Right away you could tell Ms. Rasiniack had a passion for teaching and a passion for her students. Amanda loved her, and really strived to make her teacher proud. Amanda's attitude toward school changed because of the influence of Ms. Rasiniack. About halfway through first grade, Amanda informed us, "I want to be an elementary school teacher when I grow up."

First grade was Amanda's launching pad. She excelled in school from then on. She went on to get her master's degree in (you guessed it) elementary education. Amanda set her goal at an early age and she never wavered from that goal – all because of one teacher who took the time to care.

I often think about Ms. Rasiniack and wonder if she ever knew what a positive impact she had on Amanda. I do know that when we moved away from that school when Amanda was in 2nd grade, she and Ms. Rasiniack remained pen pals for many years.

If you have an opportunity to teach or coach, never underestimate what an opportunity you have to lift a young person up and help them grow.

Keeping your dreams alive

"I want to live on a lake."

Early in our marriage, we used to vacation in rental houses on a lakefront in Wisconsin. We loved our time there: fishing, spending time on the water or in it, and just enjoying the lake view. We enjoyed those vacations so much that together we decided we should live on a lake. We shared our dream with friends. Some of them said it was not a good idea, or warned us that we would never be able to afford it. We didn't buy into their doubt, though. We started investigating our options and looking for place to live up in Wisconsin.

Our interest in relocating to a lakefront community was not just vacation-oriented. We were looking for a good place to raise our kids. Where we lived in the city did not have many good public-school options and crime was on the rise. We wanted to find a safe place to raise our children, three of whom were girls.

As we searched, we found that Wisconsin held many lake home opportunities, but not many job opportunities for a career IT executive like me. Sure, there were plenty of opportunities if I were in the trades, like carpentry or electrical. But handy, I was not. We weren't having much success locating our dream house.

Rather than give up on the dream, my wife suggested, "Maybe we can find a home on a lake closer to Chicago? And you can commute to work?" We turned our search in that direction, but ran into more dead-ends as it seemed that the homes we liked were out of our price range. At the other end of the spectrum, the homes we could afford needed way too much work, or weren't really "lakefront" homes. We changed our search strategy again, and expanded our search to further out of the city. One day, we found a lake and home we liked.

I wasn't sure whether the home listed at $125,000 was priced right, and I asked a good friend Jamal who knew real estate to take a look and give me his opinion. Jamal reviewed the listing, the house and the property, and came back to give me the bad news. "Larry, the house is not worth $125,000." He then added, "But it's hard to put a value on having a lake in your backyard. I think it's a great buy."

With that encouragement, we put our money down and purchased that home. The day we closed on the house, my wife and children and I were so excited that we drove out there and spent the night there – sleeping on the floor of *our lake house.*

We spent 15 great years in that house and raising our children. We spent the summers swimming, fishing, or boating on that lake. Winters, we enjoyed ice skating and hockey.

Plenty of people spoke up to discourage us, but we never gave in to the admonitions that we could not afford it or did not belong in a lake house. We made our dream happen, and we raised our family and became empty nesters in that lake house. While it was true that we did not end up in a Wisconsin lake house, the Universe conspired to help us make our dream happen in another way.

The Universe guides
the way to school

"Maybe we should just send the kids to public schools?"

When we lived in the city, our children attended the Catholic school near our home. While there was a significant cost in sending our children to Catholic schools, we felt it was a good investment in their futures – the quality of education was better than we could find in the public schools, and it gave the kids a chance to grow in the faith, too. We had been active parents in the school – I coached baseball and was involved with the parents' club, and my wife served as a teaching assistant.

When we made our decision to move to the lake, we checked out the public school system there and found that it had high ratings, in fact one of the best in the state. While sending the kids to Catholic schools in the city was a "must," we felt that we could take advantage of the high-quality public school system near our new home. It would save us a significant amount of money, and we figured we could continue the children's religious education by sending them to religious education classes (CCD or Confraternity of Christian Doctrine). Our plan was in place, we thought.

When the news got out that we would be moving, our Catholic school's principal, who was a Springfield Dominican nun, came up to me and said, "I heard you and your family are moving. We're sorry to lose you, but I have great news. We have a Catholic school in the area where you're moving." I didn't comment, not wanting to tell the principal that we weren't planning to send the children to Catholic school once we moved. I told my wife about the conversation and we figured that would be the end of that.

A few days later, I got a phone call. On the other end of the line was the principal of the Catholic school near our new lake home. She introduced herself, also a Springfield Dominican nun. The principal said, "I heard your family is relocating here. Why not come out on Sunday and I can give you a tour of the school and campus?" I told the princpal I would let her know.

My wife and I talked it over. We agreed that it wouldn't hurt to at least take her up on the offer of a tour. Maybe this is a sign we should be sending them to the Catholic school? We ended up meeting with the principal, who gave us a tour. We liked what we saw. We also talked with her about our family traditions, how my parents and my wife's parents each sent us to

Catholic schools – even when they had tight budgets, like we did.

When the conversation got around to the topic of tuition, we found that the cost at this school was more affordable than we had anticipated. My wife and I talked it over, and when we moved to the lake home, off the children went to the Catholic school.

It turned out to be a good thing for all of our kids. It gave them a great foundation of faith, and their academic accomplishments in Catholic schools and in higher education proved to be a great value to them. While we may have spent more on their grammar school education, those investments in our children paid off when they earned grants and scholarships to attend the colleges of their choice – due in great part to the good grades and education they acquired in parochial schools.

I learned the importance of paying attention to opportunities that present themselves unexpectedly. Often, those opportunities might just be the Universe working to take care of a need, even if in a different way than we expected.

Putting material things in their proper place

"How does it feel to have reached your dreams at age 35?"

For years, we held onto our dream of living on a lake. We saved, we searched, and in June of 1985, we made that dream come true when we moved into a fabulous house – on a lake, just as we'd dreamed. The town seemed perfect and life seemed perfect. It would be an understatement to say that we were excited. We'd registered the children in a good school, and I was able to keep my job and commute into the city each day for work. Everything seemed perfect.

To celebrate our new home and to share it with family, we planned a Fourth of July cook-out. The day was sunny and the house was full. We were riding high about how great things were going: the new house, a great work arrangement, the kids in a good school. Our lives were going great.

One of my sisters-in-law walked into the kitchen and said, "This house is just beautiful. How does it feel to reach your life's dream at the age of 35?" I was excited about the comment for a few seconds. But when I thought about it more deeply, that statement hit me like a punch in the stomach.

Is this all there is, I thought? We had reached the dreams that we had been chasing for a long time. Get a good job (check), find a great wife (check), start raising children (check), and buy your dream house (check). Now what?

It was in that moment that I realized we had been chasing material things. I'd thought that once we acquired these magical, beautiful things, life would be perfect and I would be happy. Sure, it felt like an achievement to have acquired things I wanted – like the lake house – and for a moment, those things made me happy. But something about my sister-in-law's comment woke me up to something I'd known all along: there had to be more to life and happiness than gathering material things.

For the first time in my life, I realized there needed to be more. While material things can make life more pleasant, there must be some other purpose for us on this earth. Even with a great job, great family, beautiful lake house, I still felt empty and incomplete.

Then I started to search. I wanted to understand why I felt incomplete. In that search, I came to realize that there was a spiritual side of me that was missing. The more I learned, the more I wanted to strengthen the connection to my source. In me grew a burning desire to be helpful to other people.

I began to recognize myself as a spiritual being having a human experience. I began to see that there is so much more to life than gathering material things that society says are supposed to make us happy, or acquiring possessions that make other people envious and think you are happy. I found that happiness is an inside job – not based on what you have accumulated and always based on what you have done to give back, to help others reach their true potential.

The best way I've found to fulfill my spiritual needs is to be of service to others. Whether that service is coaching youth sports, helping my children reach their personal goals, mentoring a coworker on the job, or helping someone find their way out of tough situation. I've learned that my gift is to pay back what's been given to me. The interesting thing I've found: the more I give back, the more I receive in return.

Little did I know that simple compliment like "How does it feel to reach life's dream at 35?" would wake me up to my true life's purpose and lead me on a spiritual journey that's been going strong for more than 30 years.

Material things are not what bring us true happiness. Happiness is the byproduct of doing the next right thing. I know that sounds simplistic, but take some time and marinate in that thought. Think about the times when you helped someone out without expecting anything in return, and the warm and fulfilled feeling you get. That's the feeling I search for each and every day. Try it for a while and see how it works out.

Reaching for your highest moral values

"Give me some dirt on your boss."

A while back, I was part of a company that went through some major management changes. I had been with this company for many years and had worked for the same manager, Ken, for all of those years. During that time, he wasn't just my manager, but also became my mentor. We ended up being close friends.

With the reorganization, a new group of young managers took over. Not long after this new management team came in, I was called unexpectedly into the VP's office. He got to the point pretty quickly.

The VP told me he felt I was ready for a promotion. He said he could help me get that promotion. All I had to do was give him information about my current boss – who was also my mentor and my friend – about anything unethical he had done. The VP's intent was to fire my boss and move me into his position. I was very much surprised and taken aback by this offer.

I explained to the VP that my boss had never done anything unethical and as a result I would have nothing to give him. I didn't stop there. I told that VP that even if I had information, I would never give it to him – because a year from now, he would be calling in someone who worked for me and offering them the same deal.

This VP played a card and I did not cooperate, and that just would not be tolerated. While I was able to keep my integrity and my loyalty to my friend, it was career suicide for me at that company. From that point on, I was a marked man at that company. Over the next two years, I was basically in limbo: raises and reviews got knocked down or changed, and I would never receive another promotion.

I had been at that company for 12 years, and I had always felt I would be there for my entire career. The job was not going well, and it was obvious that it was time to move on. I was in a daze and honestly feared for the future. I had young children at home and needed to provide for them. I felt trapped and like I had no options.

A job search eventually yielded another opportunity, though. I was finally able to land a new job and left the company where I thought I'd spend my entire career. The day it was announced I was leaving, I got a major surprise. On the same day, I had two *different* companies call and offer me a job.

Here I had been, walking around in a daze for two years and fearing that I was trapped, out of options, and unemployable. The whole time I was afraid I was out of options, there were actually opportunities just on the other side of that fear. It also helped me realize my worth, and recognized there were other employers who would be interested in my work and would value my contributions

As is the case with most every major forced change in my life, it was always better on the other side of that change. After I left the old company, I had a much better job and more satisfaction in my life. I realized that I had wasted a lot of time worrying when worry wasn't necessary. Never again did I fear for my future. I came to regard worry as a waste of time and a lack of faith.

My manager Ken and I are still friends. It was fun this year calling him on his birthday and watching him try to figure out FaceTime.

Admitting I was powerless

"I don't know, maybe it's alcohol related."

In the fall of 1986, I was at an emotional low. I don't know if it was a midlife crisis or something else. We had just moved to a new lake house; that was supposed to make me happy. I had a great family; who wouldn't be happy about that? I had a great job; which brought satisfaction but not happiness. Despite all the great things going on, I felt like I was at an all-time low.

My drinking was not any heavier than it had been in the past, but that warm feeling I used to get from a beer was gone. I used to be able to go out for a couple drinks and have a good time... but not anymore. When I was out at a pub, I knew I should be home. When I was home, I wanted to be out having a drink. I felt like I didn't fit anywhere.

I couldn't figure it out. I felt like I had accumulated all the things I needed to be happy, but I wasn't happy. I didn't know where to turn. I was as emotionally low as one can get, so low that I was even considering suicide. Not seriously, but the thought did cross my mind.

I considered whether I might be an alcoholic. I felt like I'd worked hard *not* to be one. I'd quit hard liquors even before I was legally old enough to drink, and all I drank for 16 years was beer. In my mind, if all you drink is beer, you are not an alcoholic. It was true that I got drunk a lot, but that's what hard-working people did, right? They earned the right to blow off a little steam. At least that's what I thought.

But I was at a crucial "jumping off" point, and I needed to find some answers. My wife Debbie suggested I talk to one of my older brothers, Dennis, which I thought was a good idea. Dennis had quit drinking a few years prior, but that's not why I agreed to talk with him about my drinking. I reached out to him because he was the only single brother I had. If he thought I was crazy, he wouldn't be able to tell a sister-in-law what a crazy brother-in-law she had. So I called my brother.

I remember that chat with Dennis quite well. I poured my heart out to him about all these crazy feelings I was having about being unhappy even with so much good in my life. At one point, I casually (and cleverly) slipped in a mention of: "I don't know, maybe it's an alcohol issue." When I said it, I watched him closely to see how he'd react. I felt like if he *did* think

I had an alcohol problem, he would have jumped all over that. But he did not react.

I was relieved by his silence. Even though I knew that alcohol and drinking was no longer fun, it was a familiar part of my routine. I couldn't imagine *not* having it in my life. My relief was bolstered by a feeling of pride at how I had been so clever in working it into the conversation.

When I left my brother's house, I was feeling much better about myself. They say, "A problem shared is a problem halved," and I felt good about getting those feelings out in the open. Dennis followed up with me the next day. I got a call from him and he asked how I was feeling. I told him enthusiastically that I felt 100% better, and thanked him for giving me that time and listening. His next sentence saved my life.

Dennis said, "I was talking to my 12-step sponsor today and mentioned that my brother thought he might have an alcohol problem." My first reaction was, "Oh no, he *did* hear me mention alcohol." I replied, "No, I really don't think it's related. I'm fine."

My brother said, "You did mention it, so you must have some concern about it. My sponsor suggested that you might want to attend a 12-step meeting with me later this week."

I did agree to attend that 12-step meeting, but not because I thought I had issues. I thought maybe my brother would get recruiting points or something if he got someone to attend. I was just trying to help him out. But I can say I was nervous walking up his driveway. I was thinking, "Larry, what have you done now? You've really overreacted this time."

My drinking pattern wasn't *really* a problem, I'd been telling myself. Sure, I would get wasted and do stupid stuff, and then commit to myself not to overdo it again. But as I got further and further away from that last episode, I would again start thinking I was okay, that I could handle just a few beers. And the cycle would repeat.

It's safe to say that this meeting changed my life. As the meeting started, each person took a turn sharing their stories and how they got here. Paul (the first guy who spoke) talked about not having many physical hangovers, but many emotional hangovers. I saw myself in his story.

As more and more people shared their stories, I found myself relating so much to what they were saying. I saw myself in their stories so much that I suspected this must be a set-up, and that Dennis had shared my story with the others in some kind of "briefing meeting" before I arrived. When it came my turn to speak (being the clever guy I am and thinking I had this all figured out), I said, "It's obvious Dennis has told you a lot about me." The roar of laughter from the room was deafening.

One of them said, "Dennis has told us nothing about you." It was then I realized I was no longer alone. By the grace of God and a lot of help from others, I have not had a drink or used a mind-altering substance since that meeting.

If you put out a request to the Universe for help, it will come, and sometimes in ways you might never imagine.

Delaying the start of dating

"**Y**ou'll have to give the bracelet back."

When our oldest daughter Melissa was in fourth grade, a boy in her class really liked her and thought it would be a good idea to give her a bracelet as a gift. This was in fourth grade, mind you. When I got home from work, she was so excited to show me the bracelet the boy had given her.

I told her it was very nice, but she would need to give the gift back. I told her fourth grade (when kids are all of nine years old) is way too young for boys to be giving gifts to girls, and for girls to be accepting them. Our discussion went on for quite a while, with my daughter trying to convince me to let her keep the bracelet. But I was firm, and the following day she thanked the boy, returned the bracelet and told him, "I'm sorry, but my dad is making me give the gift back."

As it turned out, the fourth-grade bracelet-giver had an older sister who was in my son's seventh-grade class. She began giving my son a hard time about my daughter returning the bracelet her little brother had given her. When you're in seventh grade and a girl is giving you a hard time, it is a big issue. My son came to me and asked about my reasoning for making his sister return the bracelet.

I explained to him that at some point in time, girls and guys start dating, which moves on to more serious relationships. That's unlikely to happen with this fourth-grade boy, I told my son, but eventually it's going to happen. I told him that my objective as a father is to delay that "start" for as long as I can, and fourth grade is way too early to start. My son looked at me and said, "That makes sense." He was very mature for his age.

Fast forward to today, and this same daughter who was upset for years over me "making her give back the bracelet" now has a daughter of her own. Now it's a different story. Now that Melissa has daughters of her own, she understands the lesson I was trying to teach her back when she was in fourth grade. Melissa is holding her daughter to the same standards I held her to.

Making the right decisions as a parent will often result in protests, and sometimes tears, from the kid who's the subject of that "right decision." Do what you know is right and go with your instincts, regardless of the outside pressures. Our objective as parents is to lead and guide, even when the child disagrees.

Discovering that failing is part of learning

"Can you get your sixth-grade girls ready to play against seventh-grade teams?"

The Catholic grammar school our children attended had no budget for sports programs. Not only were they missing out on physical exercise, learning about teamwork, and experiencing competition, without a funded and supported sports program, these kids would be at a disadvantage when they got to high school – wanting to play sports and having no playing experience. The public schools in the area, on the other hand, were able to pay their coaches within well-funded sports programs. When our son Larry entered high school, only one of his teammates from his grammar school made the basketball team. I started thinking of ways I could help.

My opportunity came when my oldest daughter Melissa got to sixth grade and decided she wanted to play. I didn't know much about basketball, but I volunteered to coach her team. I felt I could at least get them a little exposure to the sport so they wouldn't be at such a disadvantage going into high school.

I called Bob, the volunteer athletic director who ran the sports programs at our school, and told him I wanted to coach the sixth-grade girls basketball team. There was a long pause and Bob said, "I'm sorry, Larry. We didn't think we could find a coach, so we told the league we wouldn't have a sixth-grade team this year."

I said I understood. I told him that my daughter and some of her sixth-grade friends were interested in playing, even if we couldn't compete this year. Could I get some gym time for them so we could start practicing to get ready for the seventh-grade season the following year? Bob agreed to give us time in the school gym.

On a Thursday night about a week later, I got a call from Bob. He said he had a problem that maybe I could help with. He said our school was on the league's seventh-grade schedule, but our seventh-grade team had fallen through. Bob asked if I would be willing to coach our sixth-grade girls and have them play the seventh-grade schedule. I said, "Sure! Why not?"

I figured that our sixth-graders playing against older seventh-graders would probably get beat at most if not all of their games. But the experience they'd gather would help prepare us for the following year.

Bob said, "Great!" and then dropped another surprise on me. "You have your first game on Saturday," he said. Mind you, this was Thursday night. We'd have time for at most one practice before putting our sixth-grade girls up against their older more experienced competitors. I sent Melissa to school the next day with instructions: tell any girl in her class who wanted to play basketball to be at the gym at 5:00 p.m. on Friday for our first practice. And then be ready for our first game on Saturday morning.

Friday afternoon I walked into the gym and found eight bright-eyed girls eager for their first basketball practice. I was nervous and didn't want to let them down. I'd only played on two organized basketball teams my entire life, and I've admitted to not knowing much about the strategy of the game or even how to design a play. I did have one advantage, though. I felt like I could relate to the kids feeling nervous and fearing failure as they were trying to learn a fast and competitive sport where things can be confusing for a new player. My team and I were in the same boat.

I started by asking the girls if they had any questions. What followed was a 45-minute full-court press, the girls peppering me with questions like: "What is a double-dribble? What is traveling? What does a foul mean?" They asked question after question. The good news is that I had answers for most of their questions. I had no idea how to draw up a play, but I did know some of the basic rules.

We managed to show up for our first game on Saturday morning. As expected, our sixth-graders lost to their seventh-grade opponents. There was a bright side, though. Our girls kept it a close game. They held their own against a team that had been playing together for a year, against players who were all a year older. Even though we lost that first game, I could see the girls were surprised at how well they'd done. We all felt encouraged that we could actually be competitive at the next level up. We continued to practice and play. We continued to compete and get better and we finished the year with a .500 record. It was quite an accomplishment, considering our lack of experience.

The following year, our girls were now playing against opponents of their same age level, along with having a season's experience playing together. We did much better than I'd expected. By "much better," I mean those girls never lost a single game in seventh grade. We may have taken our knocks that first year, but being willing to fail by playing a more difficult schedule really paid off for our team. It also helped our team members have higher expectations of themselves because of the positive results that first year.

This willingness to risk failure became an important part of my coaching plan. I never wanted my players to fear failure, and I always wanted them to have fun. I watched too many coaches from other teams harshly calling out children for their failures. My coaching philosophy was that when one of my players made a mistake, she already knew it. So why bring it up in a way that shamed them? I allowed the girls I coached to make mistakes, and fail if necessary, without consequences.

Coaching not only gave me the opportunity to help my daughter and her team learn about basketball (as I was learning alongside them), it also taught us some life lessons as well: Don't back off of a challenge for fear of failure. There are no failures, just learning experiences. I appreciated watching these young people mature, and helping them learn how to work together as a team. I learned as much as the girls did about the importance of overcoming challenges and facing failures on the road to winning.

These lessons proved themselves to be true. A couple years later when these girls went to high school, every one of them made the girls basketball team.

Pushing ahead with good ideas

"A small forest gave its life to print these reports every night."

I took a job as an IT manager at a small manufacturing company in the northwest suburbs of Chicago. One of our nightly tasks was to print reports that were used by people in various departments in the company. The reports summarized the previous day's production performance and helped departments make business decisions about operations for the current day.

Printing all those reports required a huge amount of paper. We probably produced 20 to 25 boxes of paper reports every night. I could see pretty quickly that this process wasn't sustainable. Paper was expensive, as was the wear and tear from running our printer equipment so hard. The process was also bad for the environment. All the paper we used probably required a nice-sized forest be mown down each week.

In a previous job, our information technology group reduced its paper consumption by implementing an online viewing system for much of the report output. Our customers could get to the information they needed quickly by viewing report data online at a terminal at their desk. The data would be stored online if customers needed to review it later. They could print only the parts of the reports they needed, rather than paging through five boxes of paper and then throwing most all of it away. This online system saved my previous company time, money, and many, many trees. I saw an opportunity for my new company to take advantage of these same improvements in efficiency and cost-savings. When I took the idea for online reporting to the managers whose departmental reports we were printing every night, I ran into one stone wall after another. Often I heard, "That's a nice idea, but my customers need the hard copy of those reports." I must have approached five or six of the managers, and got the same response from all of them. Maybe it was fear of change?

When I realized I would not get company-wide buy-in, I shifted gears to see what improvements I could make on a smaller scale with reports produced only for my area of responsibly. I found that of the total number of reports, about 10% were being printed for my own department. Not a huge opportunity, but at least it was a start. On that basis, I put together cost justification and a three-year ROI (return on investment). I obtained approval to purchase the online reporting package for my group.

We saw great results right away. My staff was able to find the information they needed with a quick online search, rather than digging through stacks of paper reports. We saved the time previously used to print our reports, reduced my department's paper consumption, and saved the wear and tear on our printers. In addition, my staff would often have to look up historical data from a previous day. In the past, that meant pulling out stacks of paper that were stored by date, and then paging through that stack looking for the particular report. With the online reporting system, it was a simple search that took a few minutes at most.

To keep people informed, I would host quarterly presentations to my customers and management, updating them on changes and progress being made in our department. In one of those presentations (not long after implementing our online reporting package), I outlined our new system and highlighted some of the benefits we had already realized.

After my presentation, a coworker approached me. Audrey's department was one of the biggest users of the paper reports we printed every night. Audrey would show up at the distribution center every morning with a shopping cart, which she would load with four or five boxes of reports before heading back to her area.

Audrey said, "Tell me a little more about that online viewing program." The more she learned about how the system was improving the operations in my department, the more interested she became. "Can I start using your online viewing system?" she asked.

I said sure, let's work together to get this done. Without going through managers as I had in the past, I instructed my staff to work directly with Audrey and make her department's reports available online. The changes took a few days and then her printed reports were now online, she was up and running, and we were saving an additional four or five boxes of paper a night. No more shopping carts full of paper for Audrey. About a week later, my shopping-cart friend (who no longer needed her shopping cart) ran into her coworker Margaret in the cafeteria,

Margaret was also a regular at the IT distribution center, lining up each morning to load up with two or three boxes of printed reports. She asked Audrey, "How come I haven't seen you picking up your reports every morning?"

With a bit of excitement, Audrey explained why: online report viewing, faster, less expensive, less waste. Margaret called me and asked if her department could also use the online system... and we had another convert, and we were quickly saving another two or three boxes of paper a night.

Word started to travel fast. Almost daily, I was getting another request for online report viewing. To keep the momentum and excitement going, I crafted a challenge board to display in the distribution center. We put a posterboard up on an easel and drew a thermometer on it. We assigned each department their own color marker, and let each of them fill the thermometer with their department's color as they reduced paper use. The departments began competing with each other to see who could save the most paper.

The original project estimate showed us recovering the cost of the online viewing system within 36 months. But with so many of the company's departments buying in, we actually recovered the cost of the company's investment in less than seven months.

New ideas and processes don't always get support right away. People get comfortable with the status quo, and are famous for saying variations of, "But we've *always* done it this way." You never know where the support for a new idea will come from, but you're likely to buy-in from people who are closest to the work. The important thing is to share the knowledge with all those involved, not just with management.

Also, getting a "no" doesn't need to be a showstopper. You can always find another angle to make your case, and gather support by showing tangible benefits that other people will get excited about.

Walsh Family, Christmas 2018.

Overcoming objections

"But we've always done it this way."

As a new IT manager at a small manufacturing company in Chicago's northwest suburbs, I was always on the lookout for ways to make things run more smoothly or make people's jobs easier. After we'd found ways to reduce our printing costs by making reports available online, I looked for other ways to improve operations at the company.

At a point in the history of information technology, large amounts of data were stored on removable tape reels, which had replaced punch-card input and really improved efficiency. However, as time went on and technology improved, those tape reels could slow down the nightly production process. Tape reels involved a lot of manual labor in the mounting and unmounting of tape, and had the potential to introduce errors in processing. Our department had a goal to finish processing and have updated data ready for our customers by 5:00

a.m. each day. When I first asked my new staff why we were always missing this goal, I was told the 5:00 a.m. goal was not realistic. I later found out that manual intervention and tape failures were two of the primary reasons we seldom reached our daily goal.

I had been part of a project at a previous employer where we moved the majority of tape data over to online storage devices. The previous company was able to reduce processing time, realize fewer data errors, and improve reliability by moving from removable tape storage to online data storage. As I had done with earlier proposals to reduce our paper costs, I took this idea to other managers. Like before, they had plenty of objections. "We need these tapes for the security of offsite storage" or again the old stand-by: "This is the way we've always done it."

I had responses ready for the objections. For example, if they felt more secure keeping tapes off-site, we could load the data into online storage at the start of the process. After processing was complete, we could move the online data back to tape. With this method, we could use one or two tapes at the end of a processing cycle, rather than the 20 or more tapes we sent offsite previously. As before, the department managers were more comfortable doing things the way they'd always done them – even if that meant their morning reports were often late.

A few weeks later at a company golf outing, I was riding in a cart with Joe, one of the programmers. Joe's daily processing still used manual tapes. I talked to him about the idea of moving from tape to online storage, but I received many of the same objections I'd gotten from department managers.

As we discussed it further and I was able explain the advantages and some alternative options, Joe agreed to give it a try. I think being in the relaxed environment of a golf cart helped him consider different options. The following week, we made the changes and moved his data online. He immediately started to see the benefits. Not only did this change reduce frequent tape failures, but removing the manual intervention and time delays of tape mounts sped up the processing time so much that we cut out two hours of processing time each night. At the end of the shift, we needed to send only one tape offsite, rather than 20 tapes we'd been sending out previously. Things were going well.

Just as I'd seen when improving our online report-printing processes, the word began to spread regarding the advantages of online storage. Joe was having lunch with Ed, one of his programmer colleagues. Joe asked Ed why he was looking so tired. Ed explained he'd been awoken twice during the night by phone calls asking for his help resolving tape-based errors in his program stream. Joe said, "That's too bad.

I don't have those issues any more. I moved all my tape data to online storage." Ed wanted in on this new idea.

It wasn't long before Ed was knocking at my door, asking for help. We got him set up, moved all his tape data to online storage, and had him saving hours of processing time, as well (in addition no more middle-of-the-night calls to fix tape errors). Before long, all the programming groups had gotten wind of these successes, and were all asking for help in moving to online storage. By the time everyone was onboard, we were cutting over four hours out of processing time and reducing labor and hardware costs.

The biggest benefit to my department was that we began meeting our 5:00 a.m. deadline on a regular basis. In fact, missing our daily deadlines was now a rare occasion, where before it was a rare event to meet those deadlines.

These experiences as an IT manager showed me the importance of understanding the work other people are doing, getting a sense for what they need, so you can make your best contributions to improving things. I learned by many examples that even if you have the best ideas in the world, you'll often hear objections like "that won't work here" or "my department is different." If you believe in your ideas, don't be shy about pushing them forward. If you do, people will come around to see the value.

Taking responsibility for yourself first

"Make improvements and the money will follow."

When I took over the information technology (IT) shop in a Chicago-area manufacturing company, the department was not in good shape. They were often missing their production commitments, and as a result had very little credibility with company management. But for me, it was a dream job. I saw the opportunity, with a little effort and some practical management skills, to turn this IT shop around and make it one to be proud of.

The first thing I noticed was that the staff had really low morale. They were convinced that the reason they were missing deadlines and not delivering on commitments was because of poorly performing hardware that often failed, along with a weak management team they felt wouldn't listen, and unrealistic expectations that could never be met.

At our first meeting, I started by encouraging the team that things were going to get better from this day forward. Next, I made them part of the solution by telling them I needed their help to get this done. We then moved on to talking about our current state. I heard the typical objections and excuses: our hardware is bad, the project expectations and timelines are unrealistic, we get no support from management.

As a team, we began talking it through. The staff felt like management didn't value the work we were doing and wouldn't listen to staff input about old and faulty hardware. I asked them to look at the situation from a different angle: perhaps management wasn't showing interest in spending more money on our department because they didn't think we could deliver on our business commitments. Why would they throw good money at bad performance?

We must start, I told our team, by improving our image with management, and the only way to do *that* was to perform better with the equipment and staff that we had at hand.

We worked together to set down a series of objectives. I knew if we could accomplish these smaller, achievable objectives first, we could then start knocking down the big ones soon thereafter. I explained while it was true that our IT hardware was old and outdated, we must first improve on meeting our commitments before management would allow us to purchase new and more reliable hardware.

We started by instituting a more-frequent cleaning/maintenance program on the hardware. We focused on cleaning media surfaces on a regular basis, monitoring devices, and focusing our maintenance efforts on the devices that failed most frequently. We brought in our maintenance provider and put together a plan of action to monitor hardware that was starting to show signs of failure, and address issues before they failed, rather than in the middle of a production run.

This type of preventative maintenance might sound like an obvious approach, and it was. But prior to this, the staff hadn't been taking personal responsibility, blamed others, and did not take on the task of monitoring the systems themselves.

The improvement was almost immediate. With the added attention to maintenance, our equipment reliability improved and we actually started making some of our committed deadlines. We still had maintenance issues, but they became less frequent. As a result, the team's morale began to improve, and management started to notice. We were able to accomplish these improvements without the company spending one additional dollar on our IT shop.

Once we started meeting our commitments, the staff began to believe that maybe the schedules were, in fact, achievable. In fact, it became a challenge to them to continue improving on our commitments, rather than begging for the commitments to change. We were all proud to say that we had turned a major corner. Team members started taking ownership and displaying pride in the jobs they were doing. With everyone starting to move in the same direction, I think they actually started having fun on the job.

As we continually improved on delivery of our business commitments, we started getting recognized by management as a team working hard to meet corporate goals. Gradually, we started to gain respect, and some of our budget requests for hardware upgrades started to be approved. Management no longer looked at us as a burden, but as a team that was goal-oriented and company-focused.

While the updating of our shops processes and hardware took about three years to complete, the improvements started on day one. And those improvements started when my staff began taking pride in their work, responsibility for the things that were in their control, and not worrying as much about those things that were not in their control. We all learned the value of not blaming others, and doing what we could do with what we had at hand. When putting those lessons to work, things can't help but improve.

Standing out from your competitors

"**Y**ou've reached Lou... the most dedicated paper salesman in the world."

As the manager of a computer department that consumed lots of paper each month, I had sales reps constantly vying for my business. Every week, I'd get calls from sales people who'd lead by telling me how much money they could save me on paper each month if I just switched over to their company.

Along the way I learned that there were only a few paper producers in the United States. Every distributor purchased their computer paper from those same few suppliers, which meant they were all paying basically the same price. The typical sales pitch included a low starting price (to get my business). After I'd start using the low-bid supplier, they'd slowly raise my prices until eventually I was spending more with the "new" supplier than I had been with the old one. I'd then have to start looking for another new supplier. You can imagine that I began to get tired of this cycle.

One day I got a call from a new potential supplier who asked if he could come in and talk paper. On the phone, his pitch was open and honest. One of the first things I noticed was that he didn't sound like every other paper sales reps I'd talked to. Absent was the standard pitch of "I can save you tons of money, blah, blah, blah." He said his name was Lou, and he just wanted to talk paper. I liked Lou's approach, so I agreed to a meeting.

Our first meeting was one of the most unusual sales calls I'd ever experienced. Just like his opening pitch on the phone, Lou's approach was simple, straightforward, and honest.

He sat on the other side of desk and he said, "Look, Larry, let's be honest here. I have the same supplier as most of my competitors. We all sell the same 20-lb computer paper. Mine isn't any brighter than theirs. My paper isn't any stronger than theirs. It's exactly the same paper. We all pay about the same price. So why would you choose my company over every other company that comes in here wanting your paper business?"

"That's a good question, Lou," I said. "Why would I?"

"I'll tell you why, Larry. If our prices are all about the same, I have to do something different to earn your business. My difference is my promise that no one will out-service me. See my car there in front of your building?" he said. I looked where he was pointing and saw a late-model blue Ford that looked like it had recently been through the car wash.

"I always keep 20 boxes of paper in my trunk," Lou said as he pushed his business card across my desk. "And here is my home phone number. I know you run three shifts at your company here. If between shipments, your people ever run out of paper – day or night – they can call me. Even if it's the middle of the night, and I'll bring these 20 boxes of paper right over."

Needless to say, Lou got my business. He took the time to understand my business and what I needed. He set himself apart as a rep who wasn't selling me cheap paper – he was selling me high-quality service. He kept his prices consistent and competitive, and he gave me the reassurance that I had a backup plan in case my people ran out of paper supplies.

Another reason I stayed with Lou was because of his sincere enthusiasm and the pride he took in his work. When I'd call to leave him a message, his voice message greeting said, "Hi, you've reached Lou... *the most dedicated paper salesman in the world.* Thanks for calling. Leave a message and I promise I'll return your call as soon as possible." You knew you had a partner when you did business with Lou. I often wished Lou's company offered a wider range of products: I had other paper needs he might have supplied, but laser paper was all he sold. Looking back, I respected that

Lou was staying focused and not trying to be a "jack of all trades."

He showed me the importance of being yourself and not putting a false wrapper on who you are. Lou offered a great example of what it looked like to take pride in your work, daring to do your job differently, and setting yourself apart from your competition.

Doing your homework

"If I can't improve your business in 30 minutes or less, you can throw me out of your office."

Receiving sales calls was a regular part of my job as an IT manager. It wasn't my favorite part of the work, and I admit that often times I was a bit short on the sales calls I received. One of my pet peeves was that many sales people made the majority of their calls on Mondays. I used to say, "They must have found Christ over the weekend and now they are ready to sell."

Mondays are typically the worst days to contact IT managers, who were always trying to catch up on what happened over the weekend and planning for the week to come. To make those Monday sales calls more painful, the sales reps would often lead with the same pitch: "If I could show you how to save $1,000 a month in your paper costs, would you be interested?"

One of these sales calls came in on Thursday afternoon, with the rep giving the same old pitch about how he could save me money on our invoicing forms. I must have been having a rough day, because I cut him off and snapped, "Look, I've heard this same pitch a hundred times. You'll come in with a low bid and then jack the price later to make it up on the back end. You won't be any different than the others."

The rep kept his cool, and said, "I'll make you a deal. Give me 30 minutes of your time. If I can't show you in 30 minutes how I can help your operations improve, you can throw me out of your office." I liked his confidence, so we set up a meeting.

Tom arrived for our meeting and was clearly well-prepared. He said he had done some research on our company. He noticed that our corporate logo was in particular color blue. He even knew the "Pantone number" for our logo's blue color. Before that, I didn't even know that different colors all had numbers. He noticed while our billing forms did display our corporate logo, the logo was in black and white. Tom said, "We've found that customers have a better feel for a company's corporate identity when the billing forms include a company's logo in the corporate colors. Along with identity, providing a uniform look improves corporate branding. Tom said he could make these improvements in our billing form at no additional cost.

Tom continued, saying that he'd reviewed our billing forms more closely and noticed that the "remittance copy" (the sheet that customers tear off and attach to their payment) did not say anything about "Return this copy with your payment." He said research shows that by including this wording on the remittance copy, a higher percentage of customers actually include the copy with their payments (which helps accounts receivable departments keep track of paperwork). Tom asked for permission to speak with our accounts receivable department (AR) to verify his findings.

I was impressed with his insights, and told him that, yes, he was free to contact AR. Our AR people confirmed that this change could save them at least two hours a week, which they currently spent trying to match payments with invoices. Tom was now adding value to a simple billing form, and was thus helping me save the company money.

Tom continued to show how much homework he'd done before our meeting. He said, "My research shows that you have a lot of repeat supply business with your customers. Have you considered that if we include a supply list on the back of these invoices, which is currently blank, we can also put an 800 number on there and make it easy for your customers to reorder what they need?" He then suggested that he talk to our order entry department and get their input that this would be a good way to help increase supplies sales. Once again, Tom said we could make these updates without any additional cost.

Needless to say, Tom earned our business by doing his homework and finding ways he could help us improve our business. Rather than being one more sales reps offering nothing more than the lowest price, he helped us improve our corporate image, reduced accounting time for our AR staff, and helped increase repeat supply sales – all without any additional expense to our bottom line.

Tom got our business, and he taught me yet another lesson about the value of doing your homework, setting yourself apart from your competitors, and earning respect by partnering rather than just selling.

Don't worry what other people do

"Well, what will third shift have to do?"

The IT department I led needed some work. Morale was low and our third shift seldom made our goal of having all our nightly production processes completed on time and ready for our customers by 5:00 a.m. each morning. Our credibility with other departments was suffering, and I knew we had room to improve.

We ran three eight-hour shifts in our IT shop, with each shift having a manager. An upcoming projects required me to move our managers around to ensure the project was completed on time. This shuffling of schedules moved our overnight third-shift manager, Jim, to the second shift, working 4:00 p.m. to midnight rather than midnight to 8:00 a.m. This reassignment yielded some unexpected insights, which ended up helping us improve operations and boost morale.

A few days after our managers got on their new schedules, Jim came into my office and said he needed to talk to me about some operational issues. From his recent experience managing the third-shift data processing, he was accustomed to finding jobs lined up and waiting when their shift took over at midnight. As often happens in IT, software or hardware problems can crop up and delay the completion of processing jobs. This was often a factor in our third shift missing the 5:00 a.m. processing deadline.

When Jim moved from third to second shift, one of the first things he did as manager was to review second-shift's procedures. He found that the second-shift scheduler would begin each evening shift by calculating how many of the remaining processing jobs would take five hours to complete. She'd use that information to determine when second shift would stop its work for the evening. Her thought was, "If we do all the work, what will third shift do?"

Even if second shift completed their runs but still had two hours available to work, she would stop running jobs – to make sure third shift had work to do, and wasn't getting off easy.

I looked over some of the previous weeks' logs and saw that this indeed was the case. When the second-shift scheduler arrived that evening, we sat down to talk about how she was scheduling the data-processing jobs. She confirmed that even if there were several hours remaining in their evening shift, they'd stop work at a point where third shift would have five hours of work to do. I asked for her reasoning behind her scheduling decisions.

She said, "If we do *all* the work, what will third shift have to do?" Whether she thought she was being equitable or she was not wanting to make third shift's job too easy, knocking off early was hurting our entire department's productivity, and morale. I explained that keeping second shift idle for hours every night was costing the company in productivity, and consequently many thousands of dollars a week. Had second shift worked their full eight hours consistently, third shift would have a better chance to deal with any glitch in processing (and we had many). Had second shift worked at their full productivity, we would likely have hit more of those 5:00 a.m. report deadlines that we were now so frequently missing.

We agreed that the scheduler's job description did not include worrying that another shift would have less work than your shift. I pointed that out to her and said, "Don't let your own performance fall short because you're worrying about what other people are doing. Make sure you're getting the best out of your own shift."

After our conversation, second shift was consistently more productive, third shift had more time to deal with glitches and final steps to get customer reports ready. We started hitting our 5:00 a.m. deadline more consistently. As a consequence, morale began to improve and our reputation with other departments started to improve.

The work being done by other shifts should have been of no concern to that second-shift scheduler. She committed to doing eight hours of work a day. Her work agreement said nothing about "I'll only do eight hours of work if *they* do eight hours." Don't worry about how much work others are doing – just do your own job to the best of your abilities.

Trusting that the Universe will provide in unexpected ways

"Mom used to say that behind every dark cloud is a silver lining."

When our oldest was a junior in high school, we started looking at colleges. College is pretty costly, and even though we were in a middle-class bracket with enough income to get by, there wasn't much left over to cover the added expense of a child in college. According to government criteria for financial aid, however, we made just enough *not* to qualify for assistance.

Around that time, my older brother John had gotten involved in a fast-food restaurant franchise, and was doing pretty well at it. I began looking at the franchise as an opportunity to make some additional money to provide for the kids' college. My wife Debbie was not fully sold on the idea, but after we both had a long discussion with John, we decided to go ahead with it. The restaurants were doing well in other parts of the city. Our restaurant would be the first in our part of town, and we hoped it would also do well.

The plan was for me to keep my day job as an IT manager, and work the store on nights and weekends. Debbie would run the store during the day. To finance the venture, I took money out of my 401K retirement funds and we took out a second mortgage on the house.

After typical construction delays and many cost overruns, we opened our doors right before Thanksgiving 1992. From the start, business was tough. Our location just wasn't ready for the type of fast food restaurant we had. We tried all kinds of things to get business to pick up, but nothing was working. Labor is important in a service business, and we learned that finding and keeping trusted employees was a hard task.

The stress started to mount. Despite our best efforts, the restaurant was not turning a profit. Between my day job and my evenings and weekends at the restaurant, I was sometimes working as much as 70 hours a week. Debbie was putting in very long hours, as well.

Not only were we not earning extra money for the kids' college, the pressure was beginning to take its toll. We didn't know where to turn, but the answer eventually became clear. In order to save the marriage and our family, we knew we had to pull the plug on the business. Eleven months after opening, we made the difficult decision and closed the restaurant.

It was an emotional day for all of us. We had poured our hearts and souls into this business for over 18 months. We felt like we were giving up our dream. To add to the misery, folding the business also meant losing our life's savings up to that point, as well as an additional $40,000 we owed on a second mortgage.

We had opened this business in the hope of making enough money to send our kids to college, but instead we lost almost everything. My mother always said, "Behind every dark cloud, there is a silver lining." At first, we just couldn't see any silver linings in this experience. But a few began to emerge.

For starters, the huge financial loss we suffered put us into a lower income-tax bracket. Where before, we were just over the income line, the children now qualified for government educational grants. Although it certainly was not how we planned it, it turned out that starting that business *did* in fact help with college costs.

I found a second silver lining. Because the lost business put us in such a financial hole, I started looking for a better job in my field of information technology. I ended up finding a job that paid more than my current job. As a result, I was able to make up all the money we lost in less than five years, and enjoyed a higher salary in the years that followed. I think about how I never would have looked for that better job if we not started that business and lost so much money. Our family held together as we weathered a bad storm, and our experience drew us closer and made us stronger as a family.

When things look dark or the road is rough, I always think back to this story and realize that it's worth putting your trust in the Universe to open doors for you, even if the silver lining around those doors might be hard to see at first.

Remembering that it's not always as bleak as it looks

"**L**et them keep the house."

We lost a lot of money when we started a fast-food franchise that failed miserably. We had borrowed money from savings and taken a second mortgage on our house. When we decided to close the business, we hired a lawyer to help us sort it all out. We got all the business bills paid off. The only thing left to handle was a renegotiating the second mortgage with the bank, which the lawyer was handling. He said if we got contacted by the bank, to direct their calls to him. We did get calls from the bank frequently, so it was a relief to have him working for us.

Renegotiating the loan took a long time. It took almost a year before our lawyer called and said he had worked out a deal with the bank, a deal he felt made sense for us. My wife Debbie and I went over the details. When we looked at the amount of money we'd be required to pay back, Debbie said she felt it was too much, and we should decline the deal.

I said, "You know, there's a chance that if we decline the deal, we might lose the house."

Debbie said, "Let them keep the house."

She said that we started out renting, and if we needed to, we could go back to renting and still survive. She said that where we lived was not as important as making sure the monthly amount wouldn't financially strap our family.

This really took me aback. I had been struggling and worrying for over a year about how we could keep the house, which I thought was the most important thing to Debbie. When she said, "Let them keep the house," it lifted a huge burden from my shoulders.

I called our lawyer the next day and told him what my wife had said. I told him we did not want to accept the current deal as the bank proposed. He warned me that if we turned down this deal, we might lose the house. I told him we were prepared to lose the house, if that's what it meant. We hung up the phone.

Our lawyer called me back a few hours later. I was expecting to hear him tell me when we had to be out of the house. Instead, he told me that when he turned down the bank's offer, they came back with a better counteroffer. The new offer was a full $40,000 less than the previous offer, and had monthly terms that we could handle.

We did not lose our house. I thank God that Debbie was flexible enough to move if we needed to. Her reasoning wasn't all about the money, but to be more practical about what was best overall for our family. I think back that if we had accepted that first offer, we might not have been able to hold onto the house anyway.

This experience helps remind me that you won't always feel like you have answers to a problem, but even when things look bleak, there's always a solution close by. I'm reminded, too, that involving your spouse in important family decisions has great benefits.

Standing up for yourself

"Mrs. Principal, I'm sorry but I earned high honors."

At a school assembly many years ago, we watched our fourth-grade daughter Beth stand up for herself. She did something I never would have done at her age, but I was proud of the courage she showed. After witnessing what she did that day, I realized that Beth would always fight for what was right and demand she got what she earned.

The children's school had informational assemblies several times a year in the gymnasium. Parents and grandparents were invited and attended if they could. These assemblies were used to update the school community on happenings in the school and to share information about any future plans in the works. It was a great way to keep people informed and involved. The agenda for the assemblies including recognition for students who had made the honor roll and high honor roll. No awards were presented, but it was reward enough for kids to hear the principal announce their names and be recognized for their performance.

The school had about 200 students. With parents and grandparents in attendance at this particular assembly, I figured there must be over 700 people packed into the gym. Student sat in chairs lined up on the gym floor, while parents and grandparents sat in the bleachers.

As the principal announced the awards for fourth grade, she listed Beth in the honor roll group. I knew this was a mistake, because Beth had actually earned *high* honors. I didn't think much about it in the moment, until I looked down into the student body to see our fourth-grade daughter working her way out of her row and heading up to the stage. Can you picture what a tiny fourth-grade girl would look like in a huge setting like this? Beth was small in stature but not in guts. I was sitting up in the bleachers next to my mother-in-law, who leaned over and whispered to me, "What is she *doing*?" I chuckled and told her, "I have a hunch she's going up there to set the principal straight."

What made things funnier was that Beth's two older sisters were in attendance – Amanda in sixth grade and Melissa in eighth grade – who I am sure were also seeing their little sister walking toward the stage, and must have been dying from embarrassment.

This little fourth-grade girl walked on stage in full view of the entire assembly, strode to the podium where the principal was busying reading off names. Beth pulled on the principal's sleeve. I watched the principal lean down as Beth whispered something in her ear. The principal stood up, nodded, and turned back to her microphone. "Please accept my apology, there's been a mistake," she said. "Beth Walsh is not on the honor roll. She achieved *high honors*." The entire assembly laughed and my daughter walked back to her seat.

I was proud of Beth that day. Not only did she work hard to earn high honors, she was also willing to risk embarrassment to make sure she was not denied her just recognition for her accomplishment. I knew in that moment that my youngest daughter would be okay in life – if needed, she would always stand up for what she had earned. She showed me the value of putting aside the fear of what other people might think, of standing up and being heard.

The days are long,
but the years are short

"I was walking away from everything I knew, into a place where I knew nothing."

We have four children, and we've been blessed that each one of them completed their college studies in a reasonable amount of time. Each of them graduated and have gone onto great paying jobs in fields they loved.

Both my wife and I are very much "in-the-moment" types of people. We seldom worry about the future or plan in great detail, having plenty of life experience that things usually work out for the best. That can be both good and bad: good, that we don't waste time worrying about bad things that may never happy; but bad, that without a plan, sometimes we get blind-sided. Dropping off our son Larry at college was one of those times that we hadn't fully prepared for, and were taken by surprise.

As our oldest child, Larry was the first of our four children that we would drop off to start a freshman year. Each one of those days was difficult and emotional for my wife Debbie and me. But with Larry, as our first, we had no idea how hard it would be to say goodbye. We hadn't prepared or planned for the emotion torrent that was waiting for us

We were excited for Larry and proud of him. He was an excellent student and as a result was able to get into a competitive program at a well-respected university. We spent time that summer helping him prepare. When the weekend came for drop-off, we packed the car with all it would carry, and off we went. The other three children stayed home, so it was just the three of us.

Once we arrived, the move-in went smoothly... boxes and bins carried up to his dorm room. It didn't hit me until we carried in the last remaining boxes. In that moment, I realized, "This is it." It was time for us to go, and we soon began saying our goodbyes to the son who had been a major part of our lives for the last 18 years. When he was born, he was the one who made us a family. He was the guy who grew up with us, as we were only kids ourselves when we found out we were pregnant. He was the boy who suffered through all of our early parenting errors.

I thought, "My gosh, where did all the time go?" They say that "the days are long, but the years are short." It seemed only days ago that we first dropped him off at preschool – and now he's off to college?

Unexpectedly, I felt the emotions starting to well up in me, as they do now as I write this. I didn't want to make a scene, and the presence of Larry's roommate and the roommate's parents gave me an "out." My plan was to give Larry quick goodbye hug in the room, and get the hell out of there *quickly*, before I turned into a crying mess. It was a great plan, I thought.

As I was feeling my emotions continue to rise, I started into my quick goodbye hug, which I would follow with a hasty exit. However, Debbie piped up, "Hey, Larry. Why don't you just walk us out to the car?" Oh no, I thought. I'm not getting out of this so easily.

It was too late by then. The dammed-up emotions were already starting to spill over. As we walked back to our car, I stayed a few steps ahead of Debbie and Larry so they couldn't see that my tears were already flowing. Not happy tears, but tears of sadness that such an important person in our lives was moving on.

When we got to the car, Debbie also realized, "Wait... this is *it*?" Now both of us were sobbing. To his credit, my son held it together. Later when I shared this story with him, he admitted his own tears started flowing as he said goodbye and walked away. Larry said, "That's when it hit me, Dad, that I was walking away from everything I ever knew, into a place where I knew nothing." It made me proud to hear him say it. He had some fear but he still took that leap. It takes a strong person to do that.

When I started the car, the radio came on. The song that came up next was "Show Me the Way," by Styx. I felt it was so appropriate, and it did nothing to slow my tears in leaving that boy at school. It's now been over 25 years, but I still cry every time I hear that song. It's a reminder to me that life goes by fast, and the best thing to do is live in the moment.

Seeking more information and not jumping to conclusions

"Where did you sleep last night?"

Larry was our only son, and was followed by our three daughters. I worked hard to keep consistent standards with the children, especially related to dating. I wanted to be the kind of dad who encouraged his son and his daughters to exercise equal levels of responsibility. It would be hypocritical, I knew, to allow my son to have sleepovers with a girlfriend, but then tell my daughters something different. I worked hard to have Larry follow the straight and narrow.

When Larry left for college, his high-school girlfriend remained behind in our home town. When he came home at Thanksgiving break, he had a chance to reconnect with her. His first night home, she came over for dinner. When my wife and I went to bed that evening, Larry and his girlfriend were in the family room watching TV.

124

When I got up the next morning, I followed my usual routine: go downstairs and let the dog out so she could take care of business. My son's bedroom was downstairs, as well. After I let the dog out, I stuck my head into his room to check on him and to say good morning. To my surprise, Larry was not in his bed. In fact, it was obvious to me that his bed hadn't even been slept in.

My first reaction was, "How dare he! Shacking up at his girlfriend's last night!" To be honest, it got me a little upset. But after a moment I started to cool down, and something dawned on me. He'd been away at college for two months, and I had no idea what bed he'd been sleeping in for all that time. I said to myself, "Give it up, buddy. Where he goes and where he sleeps is no longer in your control." I shrugged my shoulders and remember smiling at my new perspective.

Once the dog had done her business, I let her back inside. We headed upstairs together, with me still smiling about the experience that just took place.

When we got upstairs, there was my son – sound asleep, by himself on the family room couch. The joke was on me. But it showed me how if you jump to conclusions, your perception can become your reality. I had made an assumption about where my son was and what he'd done, and I really did feel all those emotions of anger and disappointment – even though nothing I thought happened ever actually took place.

A life lesson I cherished and used for many years after was the understanding that emotions can be real even when they're based in false assumptions. It's important to pay attention and look for more information before jumping to conclusions and getting your emotions churned up.

Believing that opportunities await you

"**I**t's time you found a new job."

I was four years into a new job and exceeding all the corporate performance goals that were given to me. Then I got a new boss. The two of us never really connected, and I'm not sure why. It might have been me; it might have been him. Whatever it was, we never got beyond just tolerating each other. Before long, it became apparent that one of us had to go.

The new boss took care of that when he called me into his office one day and said, "It's time you looked for a new job." He went on to say that he planned on switching the company to a new computer operating platform. My experience was not in the new operating platform, he said, so I would not be needed.

He didn't seem interested in the fact that in my 20-year IT career, I had been part of four major operating platform changes and was, in fact, the project leader on two of those four changes. But now as we got to another platform change, he's considering me obsolete?

I knew that arguing about my previous experience was useless, so I started looking for a new job. It turned out to be a blessing because my 20-plus years of working experience had made me a little older and wiser now. Before I started looking for new employment, I did some soul searching on what type of job I wanted next. I reminded myself that I was the only person who could control my job security. Here I was, having done a fantastic job over the past four years, improving the IT operations for this company, and despite all these efforts, I was still losing my job. While it was true that managing IT organizations was my "sweet spot" and I had more than 20 years of experience in that field, I didn't want to be in this situation again where someone else controlled my future. I decided that I really didn't want to go back into IT management.

As I started looking at other job options, I realized that some of the sales people who had been calling on me these past few years had a similar background as I did. They had gone to the sales side after doing the type of IT management job that I had been doing. I asked some of those people for input. Each of them said they loved the change and wished they had changed sooner. So, I started at looking at the vendor side rather than the user side of the business.

It turned out that two of my suppliers were very interested in talking to me about joining their teams, and I started interviewing with both companies. One of the positions was in sales, and required as much as 50% travel time. The other opportunity was a technical sales support position, which would require little if any travel. With our children still in grade school, I was not interested in being away from home half the time on business travel. Of the two opportunities, I seemed to be getting the most interest from the company offering the travelling sales job. It looked like my only option.

I had a final interview with them on a Friday. They told me the job would be mine and I could expect a formal offer by the following Monday or Tuesday. While the technical support job was my ideal option, giving me more time at home with my family, I was looking forward to the change and was excited that an offer was finally on its way.

For my current job, I had planned on attending a conference that Tuesday. By the end of day Monday, no offer had come in yet on the traveling sales job, so I kept my commitment to the conference. Later Monday evening, I was watching TV at home when I received a call from the other company – the one offering the tech support position that would allow me more home time. After not hearing from them in three or four weeks, I was surprised to get the call, especially late on a Monday evening. They asked if I could come in for another interview the following day. Since the conference I was attending was only a few blocks from their office, I agreed to come by for the interview, even though I had a job offer pending.

This Tuesday interview went great. I left with the interviewer telling me that they'd deliver a formal offer to me the following day. I was pretty happy, to say the least. I had gone from hanging onto a position where I wasn't being respected or value – the potential of two job offers in just a few days.

To play it safe, I planned on taking the first formal offer that came in, whether the traveling sales job or the tech support job. I fully expected that the sales offer would come in first. Yet on Wednesday, I received the formal offer on the technical position (and still no offer from the traveling sales job).

I accepted the offer on the technical support job, and the position turned out to be a great fit. I really enjoyed what I was doing, I was being valued for my skills, and the position paid more than I had been making, which let me provide more for my family.

As an epilogue, the traveling sales job offer finally did come through – on Friday, three days later than they promised. I had to tell the hiring manager I had accepted another offer. He sounded upset, but if he had kept his word of an offer on Monday or Tuesday, I would have been working for them – and being away from my family half the time. As had happened many times in my life, the Universe provided me with a better option.

I learned a few things through this experience of changing jobs. Regardless of how well you perform, your job security is *you*. The *only* job security you have is to do the best work you can each and every day, and always do what you think is right. Be proud of your own performance and be sure of yourself, which are two things others cannot change or take away from you. Sometimes the Universe knows when it's time for you to grow, and puts people in your life to facilitate that change.

Taking credit for your own work, and not someone else's

"How much does it cost to get to New Rochelle?" I once worked for a company that maintained its headquarters in New Rochelle, New York. Each year, the employees would all meet at HQ for training and kick-off meetings.

Ten of us flew from Chicago to New York on the same flight, and needed to arrange ground transportation to HQ. The only option seemed to be taxi cabs. Each cab could only take two of us. At $70 each (plus tip), the ten of us would need to hire five cabs – for a total of about $400. I was thinking there had to be a less-expensive solution. I found the transportation desk at the airport and asked, "What would be the most economical way for ten of us to get to New Rochelle?" The clerk said, "Hire a 12-person van." I asked about the cost, to which he replied, "$115.00." Compared with the $400 we would have spent on taxis, hiring a van would save $285 in travel cost.

After arriving at HQ, the CEO invited us all into his office to say hello. When we went into his office, one of the guys traveling with us (who had nothing to do with the arranging the 12-passenger van) said to the CEO, "Hey, we just saved you $285!" The CEO said, "Really, Rich? How did you save me $285?" There was a touch of attitude in the CEO's voice that Rich did not pick up on. Rich proceeded to tell him how *we* got a 12-passenger van versus taking five separate cabs. Mind you, Rich had nothing to do with this transaction, other than to ride along with us.

The CEO responded, "Rich, do you work for this company?" Rich responded, "Yes, I work for this company." The CEO replied, "Then you saved us *all* $285, didn't you?" Rich appeared to shrink at being corrected.

The CEO was 100% right: every employee must work at saving the company money. Rich learned a good lesson about not taking credit for other people's work. Myself, I learned that while other people may try to take credit they haven't earned, all I'm responsible for is making my own good decisions and performing at my best. Always tell the truth and don't try to get ahead at someone else's expense.

To thine own self be true

"If I wouldn't do it with my own money, I won't do it with the company's money."

One of my jobs required a lot of airline travel. I'd often fly from Chicago to San Francisco, and some of the major carriers charged as much as $1,400 per seat for a direct flight. However, I was able to find a smaller airline that had a connecting flight from Chicago to Phoenix and then on to San Francisco. That ticket was only $450.

To save the money, I would always book a seat with the smaller airline with its connecting flights rather than paying more for the direct flight. It was an inconvenience and added four or five hours to my trip, but I just didn't feel right wasting almost $1,000 of company money just to save a few hours of travel. My philosophy has always been: "If I wouldn't do it with my own money, then I should not do it with corporate funds."

As luck would have it, those major carriers would often honor the ticket of the smaller airline. Sometimes for both legs of my trip, and most often on the return flight, I was able convince the major carrier to honor my tickets, allowing me to fly direct while still saving my company the money. On one return trip to Chicago, despite my best begging, I wasn't able to find a carrier that would honor my ticket from the smaller airline. So rather than getting on a direct flight, I was stuck in the San Francisco airport waiting three hours for a flight to Phoenix, followed by another two-hour layover in Phoenix, getting me home at 1:00 a.m. rather than 3:00 in the afternoon.

To be productive, I got on the phone and started working with my customer base on some demos, letting me drive additional business during my airport downtime. As I was talking with one of my customers, he asked, "What's all the noise in the background? Where are you at?" I told him I was at the San Francisco airport, waiting on my flight. He said, "Really? I just talked to Tom. He and George are at the San Francisco airport, too." Tom was a coworker of mine and George was my boss.

The airline's club room had a tech area for working, and also had a bar... which was where I found Tom and George, relaxing with a couple of drinks before boarding their direct flights back to Chicago.

My first thought was "Really? I'm working hard over here while the two of you are sitting back and drinking?" I felt even more resentful when it occurred to me that while I worked hard to save around $1,000 on a ticket, they were both holding $1,400 tickets for a direct flight home. While they were enjoying a relaxing drink, I was using my time by working hard trying to close some new business.

To say the least, I was irritated and upset. That irritation didn't last long, however. I reminded myself that what other people do or how they act is none of my business. If they wanted to spend more on a direct flight, that was their choice. If they felt comfortable drinking on company time, that's their choice as well. I must be true to myself, I thought, and knew that it wouldn't feel right spending additional company funds or wasting time on the company clock.

I did get home ten hours after they did, but I felt good about remaining true to what I believed. It takes away a burden if you can avoid judgment of other people's choices, and not let yourself get irritated by what other people do.

Trusting the Universe
to help with college

"I want to go to a private university, Dad."

With four children, we knew that providing a college education for all of them would be a challenge. Our oldest two children were pursuing very specialized majors. While less-expensive state schools offered those specialized majors, it was more practical to send them to private universities. While tuition expenses at the private universities were higher per year, students had opportunities to complete their majors in the allotted four years. Some of our friends shared stories about their children going to state universities. They talked about the huge enrollments at those schools, and how four-year specialized majors sometimes took five or six years to complete because, with so many students, it was sometimes hard to get into the required classes. We felt that in the long run, because of these specialized majors, sending them to the private university would be more economical for us.

Our third child Amanda knew at a very early age she wanted to be an elementary school teacher. It was her passion. The good news for our budget was that one of the best elementary education programs was at a state university, which meant significantly lower tuition expenses for our family. In addition, with a specialized program in elementary education, the state university would guarantee that students would complete their four- or five-year degrees in a proper allotted time. It was a win-win for everyone, I thought. However, Amanda had other ideas. Amanda said she wanted to go to a private school just like her siblings had. We talked about it, and I pointed out that the state university had a well-recognized elementary education program, it was closer to home, and cost far less money. But my rationale fell on deaf ears. In the family discussion, my wife sided with my idea and also suggested a state university might be a better option. Ultimately though, and much to my financial concern, off she went to the private university.

Amanda excelled her first year at that private university. In fact, she was named the female freshman student of the year. As her first year was coming to a close, she was seeing the mounting tuition and other costs, just like we were. Toward the end of her freshman year, she called me and said, "You were right, Dad. This university might be costing too much. I'm going to apply to the state university we talked about last year." Naturally I was glad that she was considering a change to the less-expensive state school. My wife, on the other hand, said, "If she is meant to stay at that private university, something will happen to let us know that." My thought? "Sure, Debbie. Right. Maybe money will fall from the sky." Or as my father used to say, "Those are leaves on that tree in the back yard, *not* dollar bills!"

A few weeks later, not long before the end of the school year, I got another call from Amanda. She said, "Dad, I got a letter here I want to read to you." She'd received a letter from the university, saying that a university benefactor was looking for a second-year female elementary education major to work as a nanny for his three-year-old daughter. The man's wife had died suddenly and he needed help caring for his daughter. The letter said that he was very specific about wanting a "second-year elementary education major" who could handle a three-year-old girl. My daughter was one of six candidates recommended for the job.

The letter went on to say that the candidate selected would get their tuition paid, along with an additional $1,000 stipend per month. Maybe this was the money falling from the sky?

Amanda did get selected for that nanny job. For the next two years, her tuition was paid and she saved enough money to pay for her senior year of college on her own.

The benefits of that work experience have set her up for life. Not only were her college costs covered, balancing a full class load with caring for a young child taught her how to plan her schedule and be responsible. She also made connections with people through the nanny job, which helped set her up for future jobs.

Debbie had said, "If Amanda is meant to be there, and answer will come." That's exactly what happened. For as many times as it happens, I'm always surprised when the Universe shows up with what we need.

Learning lessons in a language you don't understand

"I am sorry, but I don't understand a word you are saying."

At one point in my career, I was with a company whose corporate headquarters was in Berlin, Germany. My wife Debbie and I were fortunate enough to travel there frequently for corporate meetings. On one of those trips, we purchased some souvenirs for our family back home, the types of things you'll only find in Germany, like glass dolls, fragile glass ornaments, and glass thermometers, to name a few.

Our return trip included a connecting flight from Berlin to Frankfurt, where we would catch our flight back to the US. The leg from Berlin was delayed, by about 30 minutes. When the plane arrived in Frankfurt and parked at the gate, I stepped into the aisle to let Debbie out so she could retrieve our souvenirs from the overhead storage. Some of the souvenirs were breakable, so Debbie was being slow and careful as she retrieved them from the bin. I didn't think standing in the aisle for a moment would be an issue, since it was standard practice to deplane row by row, anyway.

As I stood in the aisle waiting for Debbie to gather our things from the overhead, I heard a woman speaking behind me. At first, I wasn't even sure she was talking to me. As my wife took a few moments to gather our belongings, the woman behind me was getting louder and more insistent. Eventually she was yelling and I realized she was yelling at me. It became clear that she was not happy I was blocking her exit. I guess she had a flight to catch. I don't know, but it's safe to say she was really upset. I wasn't sure exactly what she was saying because I only know a few words of German. By the reaction of the German-speaking people around us, I assumed she was really cussing me out. I said to her calmly at one point, "I'm sorry, but I don't understand a word you are saying." She must not have spoken English, because all she did was continue fuming. Debbie was moving as quickly as she could. Since I had no clue what her issue was, we finished getting our things from the overhead bin and then deplaned.

As I look back on this event, I realize I learned a valuable lesson, which I have tried to apply to my life since then. The only reason I chose not to react to the woman cussing me out is that I did not understand the words she was speaking. As I walked off the plane, I was thinking, "I would love to be able to react this calmly even when I *do* understand what the other person is saying." The reality is that no one can *make* you upset, regardless of what they say. You make your own decision whether to be upset, or whether to be calm.

Our flight from Frankfurt to the US took off on-time, and the rest of our trip home was great. I had a hunch that German lady was having a very bad day, which might have been made worse because our arrival in Frankfurt was late. But it wasn't for me to worry about why she was angry, but only to manage my own thoughts without letting someone else's emotion disrupt my peace of mind. Being able to do this is one of the most important lessons we can learn. To me, the trick is to be able to agree to disagree without letting emotion get in the way.

Change is good despite our resistance

"I love this house... I don't want to move."

Once all the children moved out and we became "empty nesters," the house we lived in was much too big for the two of us... at least that's how my wife Debbie felt. Myself, I was very content living in that house. I loved that house. My church was nearby, my friends were close by, and we had a lake in our back yard. We had lived in that house for 15 years and raised our family there. I had no desire or intention to move.

However, my wife pressed the idea of downsizing and continued to work to get me to change my mind about moving. Debbie knew how much I loved living on a lake, and figured that if she could find a smaller house on a bigger lake, I might be persuaded to move.

She started her investigation, and finally came up with a candidate. It was a smaller house on a bigger lake, just as she'd pictured. And just as she suspected, she was able to eventually convince me that we should move.

I'm not ashamed to say it. The day we moved out, I cried – not only because we were leaving a house and an area I loved, but also because I was leaving behind the memories that were made in that house. I asked the Universe, "Why is this happening? What's the reason we're leaving this house after being here so long?" The only answer I had at the time was that I needed to be patient. I just needed to give it some time, to try and make it work.

It took me a while to find that answer. In moving to the new, smaller lake house, I found benefits that helped change my life forever and move me forward. Looking back now, I realize I was kind of stuck in a rut with my life and needed a change. At our new house, I found a new support group of friends who helped me grow and learn new things about the world and myself. I realized that things were coming into my life that never would have occurred had we stayed at the old house.

This new house needed a lot of work, and that gave Debbie and I a chance to design updates together, which brought us even closer. Because the lake was bigger, I was able to buy a pontoon boat and cruise the lake whenever we wanted. Watching sunrises and sunsets on a pontoon, with the lake looking like a sheet of glass, is something I'll never forget. It brought us closer to the beauty of the universe and what it offers if you just take the time to recognize its splendor. Later we were able to bring our grandchildren onto that boat, swimming and towing them around on a tube. The look on their faces as their tube flew in the air behind the boat was priceless. We spent many great days on that lake.

Among our new friends, I found what I felt was the most important benefit: a spiritual life that I hadn't experienced before. The people I met helped me find a life, a life that helped me grow. It's good to be open to change even if you initially feel resistance. You never know what good may come out of change.

Sometimes they just want you to listen

"I missed an opportunity to be the dad I wanted to be."

Our youngest daughter Beth was away at college when she called me one day, excited about an opportunity she was given at her university. Beth was one of four students who had been selected as a potential finalist to represent her university at a conference in Florida, all expenses paid. As part of the selection process, each candidate was required to provide the selection team a list of reasons why they would be a good candidate to represent the university, as well as the benefits the university would gain as a result of the student being sent to the conference.

I told her how proud I was of her and wished her luck during the selection process. Beth had already prepared a letter that she would present to the selection committee, and asked if she could read it to me for some feedback.

Beth's letter listed all of her accomplishments, described her passion for her chosen academic major, and detailed her plan for how she'd use the information gathered at the conference for the benefit of the university. It was an impressive letter: well thought-out and very well prepared. I told her I thought it was well written.

Beth asked for my feedback. I asked her if she knew whether this was the first year that her university had attended this conference, or had they attended in years past? She said that student representatives of the university had attended this conference every year for some time now. I suggested that she contact some of the students who had attended the conference in prior years, learn a few more details about the conference, and tie those details back to the benefits the university could expect from selecting her. I suggested doing this would deliver more-targeted, more-specific benefits for the university. She said she would think about that.

I wished Beth luck and congratulated her for being one of four finalists (out of the 50 or 60 others possible candidates at the university). About a week later, I got a call from her. She told me that she had not been selected to attend the conference. I told her again how proud I was of her, and reminded her that she should feel proud, too, just to have been considered.

I asked her if she knew who had been selected, and she said she did. She went on to say she had seen the other student's presentation, and said that the selected student had reached out to past conference attendees (as I had suggested), and gathered information that she used to strengthen her presentation to the selection committee. Beth said she felt that might have been one of the reasons the other student was selected.

Here is where I had the opportunity to be the dad I wanted to be – and I blew it. Rather than being consoling and encouraging, I went into a rant about "why hadn't she done what I had suggested, why didn't she listen, blah, blah, blah." As I continued my righteous diatribe, I heard my daughter start to cry – right before she hung up on me.

Why didn't I just listen to her, congratulate her on being a finalist, and let it go? Why did I have to elaborate on how right I was? I wish I had answers to those questions then, but I didn't.

I try to remember that when things don't go right, people often just want someone to listen and be a sounding board. They are not looking for either answers or criticism – they just need someone to listen.

Remembering that you are only as old as you feel

"I want to buy the house across the street from your sister."

My mother had an eventful life. Some would say she had a difficult life, but my mother never thought of it that way. She always stayed positive and upbeat, regardless of what was happening in her life. My mother was the oldest of 14 children, and as a result was still young herself when she took on a mothering role for her younger brothers and sisters. Many of my aunts and uncles (her brothers and sisters) told me just how much of a positive influence my mother had on their lives.

My mother married my dad when she was 27 years old, which was not typical back in the 1940s. Most people back then got married earlier, age-wise. My parents wasted no time in starting a family. Over the next 15 years, she delivered ten more children into this world. Her mothering started young, and continued without a break. Her "eventful" life continued when my dad passed away at 61 years of age in 1970, when five of us were still in grade school or high school, the youngest of us being only 10 years old. While things seemed difficult, my mother never faltered and continued her positive outlook on life.

She was 88 years old and still living on her own when she called me one day. "I have a question for you," she said. "I'm thinking of selling this house and buying the house across the street from your sister."

Can you imagine that attitude? At 88 year of age, she was still looking forward and planning a move into a new house? I chuckled and told her I thought it was a *great* idea. I said, "Mom, I hope when I'm 88, I can call one of my children and ask one of them that same question. You're an inspiration to all of us."

A funny story about that new home purchase: my brother Rich was an attorney and was handling the paperwork for her. The sellers did not make the connection that the buyer and the attorney had the same last name and might be related. When the sellers heard that the buyer (my mother) was age 88, they demanded double the amount of earnest money – they feared she might die before the purchase was completed. My mother heard about this comment and was understandably upset.

The purchase did get completed, and my mother moved into the house across the street from my sister.

After two years in the house, we heard that the man who'd sold her the house had died, and not long after, the seller's wife had passed away, as well. My mother had outlived them both... a point she made sure to tell everyone.

My mother showed us all what it means to always have a dream, and to find reasons to keep moving forward, regardless of your age. Age is just a number.

Letting people know their value while you can

"I've been diagnosed with pancreatic cancer."

Even as we were raising our own families, my brothers and sisters and I still stayed in contact with each other on a regular basis. There were ten of us, so you could expect a lot of phone calls on your birthday. I loved all those birthday phone calls... just thinking about them reconnects me back to my youth.

My 55th birthday was a little different, however. I got calls from every one of my siblings except my oldest brother, Jim. It surprised me. My oldest brother and I had a very close relationship, and he never missed a call on my birthday. I even mentioned it to my wife Debbie that I was surprised I didn't hear from him.

About three days later, I got my call from Jim. He apologized for missing my birthday, and said "he needed some time to emotionally prepare for this call." I had no idea what he meant. Jim went on to tell me that he had been diagnosed with pancreatic cancer. I was devastated to hear it. Jim and I talked for a while about how he was dealing with it. After a long discussion about how he would handle it, we said our goodbyes. Right away I jumped on the internet and looked up some information about pancreatic cancer. What I found made me cry. I read that the long-range prognosis for that kind of cancer is not good.

I shared my feelings of sadness with my 12-step sponsor, and told him just how much of a positive influence Jim had been on me. My sponsor asked, "Does he know that?" When I said no, he suggested I should tell my brother how I feel about him.

"I'd feel funny doing that," I said. "If I start telling him how much of an influence he'd been on me, wouldn't that indicate I think he's going to die?"

"How do you know *you* won't die before *him*," my sponsor said. "Wouldn't you want him to know how important he's been to you before *you* die?"

My sponsor was making sense, so I sat down and wrote my brother Jim a three-page letter. I told him about all the ways I was grateful for him: how much it meant to me that he took me along on his paper routes when I was only five years old. How excited I was when he bought me my first bicycle. How happy I was in 1963 when he gave me a shotgun for Christmas. How I owed my career to him because he got me into the computer field when I had no plans for my future. How proud I was of him as he climbed the ladder in his career and went from the mailroom to the boardroom. My letter was full of gratitude and full of emotion. I put the letter in the mail and sent it off.

A few days later, I got a call from Jim. We talked about what we meant to each other. We went over my letter point by point, and both of us cried a lot as we looked back on all those great times. It was an emotional hour – and I was so happy to get my feelings out on the table with him.

On October 1, 2005, my brother Jim passed away from pancreatic cancer. It was five months from his first diagnosis to his death.

I'll never forget the feelings of peace, walking into the funeral home and seeing my big brother lying in that casket. Our conversation from a few months before flashed through my mind, the memory of us talking through everything I shared with him in that letter. I realized then that my feelings of peace were coming from having no regrets. There were no "could-ofs" or "should-ofs" between my brother and me. Everything was out in the open. I knew that *he knew* just how much he meant to me before he left this earth.

I felt grateful to my sponsor for convincing me to write that letter and taking the risk to let my brother know just what he meant to me. I try to remember those feelings of peace, and would tell anyone who would listen: don't let time pass without letting your loved ones know how important they are to you.

Remembering your siblings as when they were kids

"It's your brother on the phone. Again."

My siblings and I have stayed close, and birthdays are an occasion to pick up the phone and send a happy birthday greeting. With ten of us, you can expect a lot of calls on your birthday. I love talking with my brothers and sisters on those calls, and how their voices take me back to when we were kids. I recall a funny incident that happened on my sister Mary Kay's birthday some years ago, which had us both laughing out loud.

As usual, I made a call to her to wish her a happy birthday. I had been busy that morning, so it was later in the day when I called her at work. Mary Kay was an RN at a local hospital and my call went through to the nurse's station on her floor. If I got lucky, my sister would be the person who answered. But this day, my call was answered by a voice I did not recognize.

I politely asked if I could please speak to Mary Kay Walsh.

My sister must have been sitting nearby, because I heard the person who answered say, "Here Mary Kay. It's your brother." The comment took me aback. How would the person know I was her brother? I never mentioned my name.

When my sister got on the line, I wished her a good birthday, and then I said, "How on earth did that person who answered know I was your brother?" She said, "Who did you ask for?" I said, "I asked for Mary Kay Walsh, of course."

My sister said, "Larry, I haven't been Mary Kay 'Walsh' since I got married 15 years ago. And you're now the fourth guy in the last few hours who's called asking for 'Mary Kay Walsh.' All your brothers asked for me the same way."

We laughed till we had tears in our eyes. I knew, of course, as did my brothers, that Mary Kay's married name was no longer "Walsh." But maybe we revert back to our childhood memories of our brothers and sisters on certain occasions? I'm not sure, but the experience gave us both a great laugh. I hope to be able to laugh whenever I can. I recommend it, because laughter *is* a great medicine.

Maintaining a
healthy perspective

"Can you imagine that from that little squirt?"

Being from a larger family has many benefits. I have learned many valuable life lessons from my parents, my brothers and sisters, and all the interactions across our family. One day a few years ago, I stopped at my mother's house to say hello. We went into the kitchen to have a cup of coffee. My mother's kitchen table was *the meeting place,* the spot we all gathered. On this particular day, on that table sat an article she'd cut out of the local paper. My mother was beaming as she handed me the article to read.

The newspaper story was about my youngest brother, Brian, and highlighted some of his achievements as the chief financial officer for the local hospital. The article gave some examples of his leadership and how he'd made a difference and improved operations at the hospital. His accomplishments were admirable and I felt a lot of pride in him as I read the article.

When I finished reading the article, I said my mother, "Wow, that is impressive."

Her response forever changed the way I looked at executives or other people in high positions. She said, "Can you imagine all that good work coming from that little squirt?"

I chuckled and said, "I'm sure the hospital's board of directors will be happy to know their CFO is a 'little squirt.'" My mother said, "Well, he is!"

To my mother, Brian wasn't a highly respected hospital executive. He was this little guy she raised from childhood. To her, he was a just Brian and the youngest of her ten children – a "little squirt." To me, he was just my little brother. My mother's perspective reminds me that it doesn't matter what position you have in life, every adult was once a kid themselves, and is someone else's little squirt. This insight has helped me often when I've had to deal with executives in my own career.

Changing your focus and watching things change

"Pull over. I need to help them."

I once read a book about a spiritual leader. One of the stories in the book described a time this man was in a cab with his assistant on the way to a speaking engagement. The spiritual leader started experiencing pain in his gut, which kept increasing until he was doubled over in pain in the back seat. His assistant realized that this was serious, and the spiritual leader's speaking engagement would have to wait. The assistant told the cab driver to take them to the nearest hospital.

As the cab driver raced to the hospital, the man's pain kept getting worse. When the cab was forced to stop at a red light, the spiritual leader looked out the window and saw a homeless family on the corner asking for help. Despite the pain he was in, this spiritual leader knew he must help. He asked the cab driver to pull over so he could give that family some money. As they pulled away from the curb and continued toward the hospital, the spiritual leader turned to his assistant and said, "That's the answer to life! As I was helping that family, my pain went away for a few minutes."

At the hospital, the spiritual leader was told that his appendix had ruptured. I have not experienced a burst appendix, but those who have say it's very painful. But despite the pain he was experiencing, when this man focused on helping another human being, his pain vanished, if only for a moment.

Changing our focus can alter the nature of a difficulty we have at hand. Even if in massive pain, focusing on helping others can take away pain for a few minutes.

Changing the need
to win as I got older

"Is winning the most important thing?"

Over the years, I have come to realize that winning is an ego-driven need, and I am for sure an ego-driven guy. But somewhere along the path of life, I changed. Don't get me wrong, I still like to win, but now I also take into consideration that if there is a winner, there also has to be a loser – and it's no fun to lose. I had an opportunity to experience that change in perspective while playing in a senior baseball league a few years ago.

Our team had an okay regular season. Our record was around .500, but we qualified for the playoffs. The playoff rule was simple: "One and done." You win, you continue on to the next game. You lose, you are done for the season. So far, we had won one game. If we won this day, we would make the final four. It was a close game and we went into the bottom of the ninth, down 8 to 7. I was on deck with runners on first and second, and only one out. We needed one run to tie and two to win it.

The batter before me hit an easy ground ball to the third basemen (the worse place on the diamond to hit it). All the third baseman had to do was step on third, and then make an easy throw to first for a double play, and the game would be over. Our team's batter was so disgusted with his lazy hit along the third-base line that he wasn't even running. This made it an easy double play for sure, and the game should have ended there.

However, the third baseman was so excited that he made a wild throw to first base. Our batter saw the bad throw, started running, and made it safe to first. Instead of "game over," I found myself at bat, with runners still on first and second, and now with two outs.

I was able to hit a hard line-drive straight at the left fielder. Fortunately for us, the left fielder misjudged the ball. He stepped in, but the ball sailed over his head. Both of our runners scored and game was over.

Our bench was going crazy as I came back in. But a funny thing happened to me that day. Sure, I was happy that we'd won, but my first thoughts were about how bad that third baseman must have felt, and the left fielder, as well. I accepted the congratulations from my teammates, but then went to seek out the other team's third baseman and left fielder. I offered my condolences, and told them they played well, tried as hard as I did, but just didn't get the breaks I had that day.

It occurred to me that this was quite a change from how I would have reacted to a win when I was younger. I realize today that we all try hard. Sometimes we win and sometimes we don't. The most important thing is trying your best.

Standing your ground

"I am sorry, but George will not be able to meet with you tomorrow."

I was in New York City making a sales call on a big Wall Street financial institution. The plan was for our VP, our CEO, and me to fly into New York on Wednesday afternoon and then have two meetings scheduled on Thursday.

I loved flying into New York's LaGuardia airport. It didn't matter day or night, the view as you approach New York was breathtaking. At night, all the bridges and the Statue of Liberty would be lit up, and the skyline was brilliant. During the day, you could observe an approach over the Hudson River, and think this time for sure the wheels would scrape the water. At the last minute, the runway would appear. Very exhilarating.

I arrived in New York around 2:00 p.m. on Wednesday, and my VP and CEO scheduled to arrive later in the day. As my cab was pulling up to my hotel, I got a call on my cell phone from the office administrator for one of the two executives we were scheduled to meet on Thursday. She told me, "I'm sorry, but George will not be able to meet with you tomorrow."

Keep in mind we had waited for weeks to get on the calendars of these Wall Street executives, and had spent a lot of company time and money on this trip. I thought about that for a moment, and then said, "I am sorry, but George must meet with us tomorrow. I am already here in the city, and my CEO and VP are already in the air specifically for this meeting. He just can't cancel like that."

I had previously been able to establish a good professional relationship with this office administrator. I think that good relationship, along with my insistence that we must meet, made her feel more of an obligation to figure something out. She said she would check with George and get back to me. The delay gave me some time to come up with an alternative plan for Thursday's meeting. I knew this was an important meeting, not only for our company, but for George's firm, as well. We had learned that they would be selecting a solution from a different company than ours, and I knew it was not the right decision for them.

I also knew George did not have all the information he needed. Once he did, he would see that selecting a different vendor was not the right decision for his company. We had been business partners for many years at this point. George's team was going to a different operating system, and George did not know we worked in that space, also. I knew I had a responsibility to George, as well as to my company, to make sure he knew that our company could be an option.

George's administrator called me back and told me that George had an emergency tomorrow and would not be in the office. I said, "Is he in today?" When she said yes, I replied, "Since I'm here already, what time can he see me today?" She again seemed taken aback at my persistence, and said she'd find out if he could see me today. When she called back, she said, "George can meet with you at 5:00 p.m. this afternoon." I said I would be there.

Both my VP and CEO were not arriving until later, so I would have to go do this one on my own. I had never met George before. I had been dealing with people in his organization who were a few levels below his position, which is why we wanted him to meet some of our executives. But it looked like that wasn't going to happen on this trip.

I got to George's office about 4:45, and was led to a conference room. As I waited, I thought how this meeting might be a stressful one – I had pushed hard for this meeting, and knew that New Yorkers are known to be aggressive, in-your-face type of business people. As such, George might not be too happy about how I pushed to get this meeting.

I wasn't wrong regarding George's response. When he walked in about 5:15 (I think the 15-minute delay was planned, to teach me a lesson), George said red-faced, "What the *hell* was so important that I had to see you today?" I could see he was fuming. I said calmly, "George, as your business partner, I have an obligation to keep you informed. You should know that selecting the other vendor as your next operating system manager is not in the best interest of your company, and will cost your company significantly more money in the long run."

"We have nothing to talk about," George said. "It's true we use your software, but from what I understand your software doesn't interface with our new system." I countered by telling George that we do, in fact, interface with the new operating system. George paused and then admitted, "I did not know that."

I replied, "George, why do you think I was so persistent in meeting with you this afternoon?" I could see him actually relax after that.

George and I went on to have a *very* productive meeting. As we wrapped up the meeting, he actually thanked me for not giving up, and pushing to meet with him even when he felt there was no need to meet. Following that meeting, the two of us developed a tremendous friendship and respect for each other, and continued that friendship for many years after that first awkward meeting.

If I felt I had a message that another person needed to hear, I had an obligation to stand my ground and make sure I had a chance to deliver that message. It is true that our company benefitted from that meeting and partnership, but George's company received much more benefit than we did. That's what good business partners do.

Showing that bigger doesn't mean better

"Your company is too small to help us."
"Why would I do business with you when I can do business with your multibillion-dollar competitor?" When meeting with potential customers, this was an objection I'd often hear.

Most of my sales career, I represented niche companies that competed against the three or four largest corporations in our space. These bigger competitors often had annual marketing budgets that were larger than our entire revenue targets for the year. I cannot begin to tell you how many times I had to deal with the "You're Too Small" objection.

Over the years I found that this objection was just like many others when it comes to sales: the objection didn't have much validity. Whether the objection was real or not, it was an obstacle I needed to overcome in order to meet my company's needs, and meet my sales quota. Even if I felt the objection had no validity, if my potential customer felt it was real, I had to come up with some simple explanation that could overcome the objection. Without a good way of handling objections, smaller companies like ours would never survive. I vividly recall one example of handling the "too small" objection.

We had an opportunity to provide a business solution to one of the larger hardware chains in the US. While they were large when it came to hardware stores, they also had significantly bigger competitors – the big box stores. One day I got a call from this hardware chain's IT director, who told me he appreciated our efforts, but he had elected to purchase the business solution from one of our larger competitors. When I asked for his reasoning, he said, "Why would I do business with you when I can do business with a multibillion-dollar competitor of yours?" I could hear in his voice he was ready to do battle, so I elected to find a better time and place to handle the objection. Since his office was local and a short drive for me, I asked if we could at least do lunch and talk about it. He agreed.

At lunch, I asked him if it was okay for me to address his concern about our company's size. When he agreed, the first thing I said was, "Bill, it's fortunate for you that the customers in your hardware stores don't have that same 'buy big' philosophy. If they did, your business would be in trouble. Let me give you an example."

I told Bill a story about when my wife had purchased a new patio set. When I set up the table and chairs on the patio, I found that three of the chairs were missing bolts. Now I had to choose a store to find replacement bolts, and I had options, as well, I told him. Two of the big box stores were close to me, as was one of the stores in his hardware chain.

If I were to follow his "go with the biggest guy" plan, I should have gone to one of the box stores. However, I thought about these big box stores and the chances of finding the right bolts, or even finding someone there who knew anything about those bolts. The odds are, I said, that I'd be helped by teenager who just started working there, and might not even know where to find the bolts. Even if I was lucky enough to find what I was looking for, I'd be unsure of the quality of the bolt, and I needed this patio set to last a long time.

I told Bill that instead of choosing a big box store, I drove to one of his hardware stores, knowing I would get much better service, and employees who'd know what I needed and where to quickly find it. Sure enough, as soon as I walked into one of his hardware stores, a clerk met me at the door. I showed him the bolts I needed, he took me straight back to the aisle with the right kind of bolts. I got exactly the bolts I needed, and had confidence that they would be of good quality.

I asked Bill if he'd agree that in this case, bigger didn't necessarily mean better? I asked him if he thought that, in some cases, bigger might mean that the customer was getting less quality and, for sure, less-personalized customer service? He agreed with me on both points.

By using an example that featured Bill's own company, I was able show him that his own objection didn't make for a good reason not to do business with our smaller company. We ended up winning his confidence and his business and we went on to become very good business partners. In fact, Bill became a great reference for me over the years. We both benefitted from our partnership, which never would have formed if I had folded on his "You Are Too Small" objection. I've been able to use that story many times over the years to deal with similar objections from potential customers.

That wasn't the only way to overcome this objection. When I'd hear "your company is too small," I would often highlight that "workload automation" is *all* we did. Those larger competitors often had many other lines of business and didn't have one area of focus – like we did. While the larger competitor might say, "Oh, by the way, we offer workload automation, too," I would show how we were different. In fact, I would tell the customer, because it's *all* we do, I would venture to say we have more people specializing in workload automation than do any of our larger competitors.

If size really is important, wouldn't it make more sense to look at the number of staff we have dedicated solely to workload automation, and compare *that* to what's being offered by our bigger competitors? Stressing that "workload automation is all we do and we have a passion for it like no one else in the business" was often enough to overcome the "small company objection," and to win the business. These experiences showed me how passion, commitment, and customer service are more important than a company's size.

Enjoying what you're doing right now

"I'd love a job that comes with four weeks of vacation."

A while back, my wife Debbie and I attended a weekend seminar designed to help people realize their potential and reach their dreams. At one point, the seminar leader sent assistants with microphones out into the crowd to ask those in attendance what their ideal job would be. The participant described many different kinds of jobs, but I heard one common theme. Many people were describing their ideal job as one "that would allow me four weeks of vacation so I could travel to places I love."

As I heard this common theme, it hit me that something was off about that desire. I thought, "Why would you want your working life to 'just be okay' for 48 weeks a year, and then spend *only* four weeks doing things you love?" It made more sense to me to make the plan to "love the things you're doing, and love what you have to do." If it's a fact that you have to work 40

175

hours a week, why not train yourself and change your focus so you also love your work? Focus on the benefits you get from the job: food, clothing, and providing for your family, just to name a few.

That weekend seminar provided Debbie and me many new ideas and lessons on how to lead a more gratitude-filled life. One of the greatest lessons was that loving what you have right now is the key to happiness. An old saying goes that "Many people live on that exotic island of "Someday Isle." Someday I'll relax and have fun. Someday I'll be able to do what I love to do. Someday I'll take time out for myself. Someday I'll spend more time with my family and loved ones. The list could go on forever.

The key to a happy life is not living in a situation you don't enjoy, and enduring all that unhappiness while waiting for that four-week, once-a-year trip to "Someday Isle." The key to life is enjoying what you're doing today, appreciating what you have and being grateful for the things in your life right now.

Living in the never-ending "Someday I'll be happy" is like standing in front of a wood-burning stove and saying, "As soon as you give me heat, I'll put some wood in you." That sounds ridiculous, doesn't it? But isn't that the same thing as saying, "I don't like my life right now. But someday, as soon as I get this or that, *then* I'll be happy"?

A universal law is that you get back what you put into something. It's not a maybe: it's a law. If you're loving life and being grateful, you'll find more things to love and more things to be grateful for. If you're struggling with life and focusing on how everything is so difficult, make a conscious effort to flip those negative thoughts over to positive affirmations.

Standing guard at the portal of your mind

The distribution of thoughts is our responsibility

I believe it was Ralph Waldo Emerson who coined the phrase, "Stand guard at the portal of your mind." When I heard that phrase, it resonated with me, maybe because of my computer background. In my view, our minds are much like computers. In every computer, the central processing unit (CPU) is where all activity starts. That CPU is where all the data is sent. The instructions programmed into that CPU will determine where, when, and how information will be processed.

Much like that computer CPU, I believe the portals of our minds work in the same way. All data or information comes in through that mind-portal. When information arrives in our minds, it has no title, no emotion attached to it, nor does it have a destination – it's just information. Much like a computer CPU, it's up to us and our minds to determine how, when, and where we process that data. Does this information mean good news? Is it bad news? Should I be happy? Should I be sad? Should I be angry? The list could go on forever. But the fact is, we are the ones who get to decide how to process that information. We can choose how to react.

Try looking back at situations in your own past; we all have examples. Think of that situation when you got upset about something, but others did not. While everyone gets the same information, people reacted differently. It's your choice on how you process the information. Work on ways to find a positive in any situation.

Another way to look at this is to think about a situation that you *thought* happened, but actually didn't occur. For instance, who hasn't heard a strange noise in the night, and experienced that pounding heart as the mind starts spinning out the worse possible scenario. It's only later that you realize the noise was the cat knocking something over, or a car backfiring outside. There was *never* any real danger, but your mind and body sure made you feel like there was.

When information arrives at the portal of your mind, you have a choice: you can determine how to handle that information. Often times, if you just pause for a few seconds and take a deep breath, you can take control of your decision. You can decide where to send that data and how to process it.

Love and acknowledgments in closing

This book would not be possible without the support, help, experiences, and guidance I have been blessed to receive over the years.

My parents Jim and Marie gave me the foundation on how to live life with integrity. From a material perspective, some would think we did not have much growing up, but the love and support they gave me was unconditional and priceless.

For their support and guidance, I'm grateful to my siblings – *all nine of them*. There is so much they all have done and continue to do for me. Here are some brief examples: Jim (RIP; showed us the way), Dennis (helped me recover), John (always had my back), Ed (RIP; family commitment), Rich (stay focused on goals), Mary Kay (the person we all go to), Kevin (calm and methodical), Noreen (keeps family together), and Brian (our caboose, but a true leader).

With so many children for our parents to keep track of, I would sometimes get lost in the shuffle. During those times, one of my brothers or sisters would recognize the gap and fill it. To this day, my brothers and sisters remain my mentors in many ways. Although it's been many years since we've lived together in one house, we continue to stay in contact and support each other as we move through the phases of our lives.

My children often times had to deal with my moods and my sometimes-immature way of dealing with things as the young parent I was. My son Larry taught me how to face my fears and step out of my comfort zone. Being our oldest child, he suffered the most as I tried to grow in maturity myself. My son was born old.

My oldest daughter Melissa kept me on my toes during her teen years. She helped me understand that life doesn't have to be hard all the time.

My middle daughter Amanda taught me that kindness is not a weakness, but a strength. Amanda helped me see the "total picture" when it comes to judging people.

My youngest daughter Beth taught me that life can be figured out if you apply yourself. She showed me how memories shared can contain life lessons.

My grandchildren have been a huge blessing to our lives. When I was growing up as a child, my parents made their share of mistakes (as we all do as parents).

I made a commitment that if I ever was blessed with children, I'd try not to make the same mistakes my parents did. We *were* blessed with children, and I can honestly say I kept that commitment and avoid some of the missteps I felt my parents made.

After raising my children, though, and gaining a little more wisdom, I realized I had made my own share of parenting mistakes. My grandchildren are my chance at a "do-over." Every day, they teach me some new lesson about how to live life without a care.

I would also acknowledge the many mentors who have come in and out of my life over the years, who've guided me both in the workplace as workers, and outside the workplace as friends.

My last and most important acknowledgment goes out to Debbie, my loving wife of over 48 years. Debbie saw more in me than I saw in myself, even before we started dating. When we first met, I was dating her roommate. Debbie told her roommate, "Stick with this guy. I'm not sure what it is, but he's got something good in him that's different than the rest."

In retrospect, I thought, "Really? She said that about *me*?" Trust me, it took a lot of deep looking to see anything special about me when I was 19 and 20 years old, acting like a foolish teen. Later, she stuck with me through some of the lowest times of my life. Who encouraged me to keep going when I really wanted to quit? Who somehow supported most of my craziest ideas? Who kept me grounded when I was ready to overreact to some perceived slight or insult? It was always Debbie.

Her patience in parenting helped us raise the mature and accomplished adults our children have become. She constantly reminded me, "It will all work out" and "let it go." Debbie's spirit has been and continues to be the ultimate example of unconditional love.

Made in the USA
Monee, IL
31 December 2020